HARDEN'S

LONDON
FOR
FREE

Fully Revised Edition

HLFF N°18057491

Where to buy Harden's guides
Harden's guides are on sale in most major bookshops
in the UK, and many major bookshops in the US.
In case of difficulty, call Harden's Guides on
0171-839 4763.

mail@hardens.com
We welcome any comments you may have on this
guide, by e-mail at the above address, or by post.

Additional research by Rebecca Lack

© Harden's Guides, 1997

ISBN 1-873721-13-7

British Library Cataloguing-in-Publication data:
a catalogue record for this book is available from
the British Library.

Printed and bound in Finland by
Werner Söderström Osakeyhtiö

Harden's Guides
29 Villiers Street
London WC2N 6ND

Distributed in the United States of America by
Seven Hills Book Distributors,
49 Central Avenue, Cincinnati, OH 45202

Contents

Introduction

What can you do in London for free?

World-famous parks, beautiful ancient woodlands, great museums, spectacular annual events and superb entertainments – the capital has an unrivalled range of free attractions.

As you will see, whatever your age and interests, whether you're a parent with children to entertain, a Londoner wanting to explore or a visitor to this great city, you really can do a lot of wonderful things here without paying a penny.

Is everything is this book really absolutely free?

Yes. Except where clearly stated to the contrary, everything in this book is free of charge. The only qualification is that if an asterisk (*) appears next to a name this means that free access is restricted in some way. The attraction may be free only at certain times (in which case the times we give are only those when there is no charge), or, in a few cases, you may not have access to the whole building.

Just in case there is any confusion, where shops, markets, pubs or cafés are mentioned, they are included because they offer great window-shopping opportunities or because we thought it would be helpful for you to know about them. Sadly, there's a charge for the goods and services they offer. Transport (Shanks's pony aside) also must be paid for. We would recommend any vistor to buy a London Transport Travelcard – they are very good value and once you have one you can zip around the capital with no regard to expense.

Organisation

How is the book laid out?

First, geographically. We've split London into six areas, starting with Central (which is mainly the area usually called the West End). The next three are West (starting at Hyde Park), North (starting at Regents Park) and South (including everything south of the river). Going eastwards, we've subdivided the world into The City (EC postcodes) and The East End (E postcodes).

Introduction and organisation

Secondly, as in England everything depends on the weather, we've divided each of the above sections into outdoor and indoor attractions. The introduction to each chapter summarises the highlights of the area concerned and tells you where you can get additional local information. We have given the most up-to-date information available, but details change and it's always a good idea to call ahead to check opening times and any other details of particular interest. If you are making a special trip, you should always confirm the arrangements that apply over holiday periods – opening hours may be modified, of course, but there may also be special events worth knowing about.

If you're interested in a particular type of attraction, wherever it is to be found, don't miss the indexes. There, we've given lists of all the museums, all the parks, all the galleries, and so on.

We hope that this book will help you to find London as fascinating a place as we continually do. And if you find something we've missed, please do write to tell us.

Richard Harden   **Peter Harden**

Londonwide
information

Introduction

A huge amount of free information about London is there for the taking. It's very difficult to find yourself far from a public library, and you don't, of course, need to be a resident of the area to go and browse through the newspapers, listings magazines and guide books.

Among the more important reference libraries are:

Westminster
(35 St Martin's Street WC2, 0171-798 2036)

Victoria
(160 Buckingham Palace Road SW1, 0171-798 2187)

Chelsea
(Old Town Hall, King's Road SW3, 0171-352 6056)

St Pancras
(opposite the railway station, NW1, 0171-860 5833)

Swiss Cottage
(88 Avenue Road, NW3, 0171-413 6533).

Westminster Reference Library also offers a chance to keep in touch with friends and relatives by e-mail and to surf the world: you can use the Internet free of charge. Bookings are taken (only) a week in advance and you are limited to an hour's use at any one time. Understandably it's very popular. Bookings: 0171-641 2034. (Time: Mon-Fri 10.00-19.00, Sat 10.00-17.00)

Away from the centre of town, consult the telephone directory to find out where your local library is – it is under the name of the relevant borough).

Libraries are also a great place to find posters and leaflets about what's going on in an area, and if you want inspiration for free things to do close to home, your branch is almost certainly the best place to start.

Locals shouldn't overlook the tourist information offices. They often have a lot of information about events that are of just as much interest to Londoners as they are to visitors. In each of the area chapters we've listed these offices.

The following services provide information on a pan-London basis.

London Tourist Board SW1
Victoria Station   2–4B
*The main Tourist Information Centre of the LTB at Victoria
Station welcomes millions of visitors every year. As a general
source of free (and other), up-to-date information about the
metropolis, you won't do better. The LTB has some branches,
which we've listed in the appropriate areas. Neither head
office nor the branches offers a telephone enquiry service –
they do, however, offer a series of premium-rate recorded
services. For a list of these call 0171-971 0026.*
/ Times: Easter-Oct 08.00-19.00; otherwise Mon-Sat 08.00-18.00 & Sun
08.30-16.00; Tube: Victoria.

British Travel Centre W1
12 Regent St   2–2C
*As its name suggests, this office near Piccadilly Circus is a
good source of information about Britain generally, as well as
about London.* / Times: Mon-Fri 09.00-18.30, Sat & Sun 10.00-16.00;
Tube: Piccadilly Circus.

London Transport Enquiries SW1
Victoria Station   0171-222 1234   2–4B
*This 24-hour telephone service is an invaluable source of help
for any queries about buses or tubes run by London
Transport. The Travel Information Office on the concourse of
Victoria Station (opposite platform 8) is an excellent source of
maps and brochures to enable you to use public transport
efficiently. There are also TICs at: Heathrow Terminals 1, 2
and 4; and at the Terminals 1, 2, 3 Underground station
(Mon-Sat); West Croydon (Mon-Sat); Piccadilly Circus; St
James's Park (Mon-Fri); Liverpool Street; Oxford Circus (closed
Sun); Euston; Hammersmith (Mon-Sat); Kings Cross.*
/ Times: office open 08.15 (Sun 08.45)-19.30; Tube: Victoria.

Disabled access
*There are three services which are very helpful for disabled
people who are exploring London.*

*General queries relating in any way to travel for the disabled
and elderly (and including information about hire of vehicles)
can be addressed to Tripscope (The Courtyard, Evelyn Road,
London W4 5JL; tel 0181-994 9294). Information about
London Transport can be had from the Unit for Disabled
Passengers (172 Buckingham Palace Road, London SW1W
9TN; 0171-918 3312) – its guide Access to the Underground
is available without charge.*

*To check access arrangements for any place of entertainment
or tourist attraction in London you can call Artsline
(54 Chalton Street, London NW1 1HS; 0171-388 2227).
Artsline also publishes a range of access guides, including
some to tourist attractions (nominal charge).*

Capital helpline
0171-484 4000

Capital Radio's all-year information line will try to answer your questions – however practical or offbeat. At various times of year, Capital also offers special helplines (numbers vary) such as revision lines (before GCSEs) and the Christmas line – a useful source of information over the period when London closes up and dies from Christmas Eve to Boxing Day. (One of the most popular lines is the Flatshare service (0171-484 8000). It is free to advertise a vacant room and lists are published in The Guardian *on Saturday or are available free from 16.00 Fri from Capital at 30 Leicester Square WC2.) Listen in to FM 95.8 for details of these occasional services.*
/ Times: helpline: Mon-Fri 10.00-22.00, Sat 08.00-20.00, Sun 10.00-16.00.

Kidsline
0171-222 8070

Kidsline is a source of suggestions – free and otherwise – of what to do with children during the school holidays. Time: Mon-Fri 16.00-18.00, school holidays: 09.00-16.00.

TNT Southern Cross

It may not be quite as comprehensive as Time Out *(which is free only on consultation in public libraries), but* TNT – *the weekly magazine for expat Aussies and Kiwis – is obtainable without any charge and has quite good theatre, cinema and other events listings. It also includes details of the many free slide shows organised by the main trekking and adventure companies to publicise their holidays. There are also articles of general budget interest, too. Pick a copy up from the publication's spiritual home – outside Earl's Court tube – or from street dispensers throughout central London.*

Ms London, Girl About Town, Nine to Five, Midweek, Chronica Latina, London Monthly

A range of magazines in several languages and aimed at differing sections of London's inhabitants (South Africans, Canadians, South Americans…) is available from principal tube and rail stations, usually on Monday mornings. As well as articles, listings and reviews they often include discount vouchers and the occasional offer of a free haircut.

London Cyclist

Try your local library for the bi-monthly magazine of the very active London Cycling Campaign (0171-928 7220, Mon-Fri 13.00-18.00). Every issue has details of social, weekend rides, and in summer, and during National Bike Week (second week in June), evening and early morning rides. All events are led and free (although some may involve trains). Volunteers at bi-monthly envelope-stuffing evenings are rewarded with free vegetarian food and the chance to swap details of potholes and near-misses with a range of like-minded people. During Bike Week there are several cyclists' breakfasts – more free grub if you can get up early enough to pedal off to join in!

The art world – *Galleries*

Especially for Old Masters – but also for almost any other form of art – London remains one of the great centres of the international market in pictures and objets d'art. Much of the business is conducted through galleries to which the public has free access.

We can't lead you to the changing artistic attractions of the capital, as many of the most interesting commercial shows last for only a month or so. Help is at hand, however, in the form of an excellent monthly publication – Galleries – of which you can obtain a copy, gratis, from almost any commercial art gallery. Its handy format contains a wealth of information, helpfully organised into areas (with maps) and indexed in every way you could possibly want (including by artist and type of work). It also contains short but interesting articles on many of the forthcoming attractions.

You could easily spend a week just exploring London's commercial galleries. As a starting point, the greatest concentrations are found around Cork Street, Bruton Street and Old Bond Street W1, and St James's SW1. There are also clusters of galleries around the junction of Portobello Road and Westbourne Grove W11, in Walton Street SW3, and to the north and east of the City.

The great auction houses are a fascinating part of the art world – details are given in the Central section.

Books

This book is a general guide, designed as an introduction to the many free delights which London has to offer. There are of course many special interests which you can pursue in London without cost, upon which there is much more information available than we are able to set out here.

The following are some of the most handy books currently in print (you can also borrow them from a library) which will give you more information.

The best, comprehensive, general guide is probably Fodor's London Companion *(Louise Nicholson, 1993). As a walking guide to London's principal architectural and historic attractions,* London Step by Step *(Christopher Turner, 1988) is both handy and reasonably detailed.* London Museums and Collections *(edited by Scimone and Levey, 1989) provides an intelligent overview, without going into so much detail as to put off the general reader.* The London Market Guide *(Andrew Kershman, 1994) tells you everything you might want to know about that colourful area of street life.*

Other sources of information

Alternative Arts
0171-375 0441
This organisation exists to provide a platform for performing artists and to reach as wide an audience as possible. For this reason, events are free and happen in public places. For details of what's on during the year send an SAE to Alternative Arts, 47A Brushfield Street, London E1 6AA – the annual calendar is available from the previous October.

Civic Trust
0171-930 0914
Heritage Open Day is a chance for the public to see, for free, buildings of historic or architectural interest that are usually closed to general enquirers. For properties outside the London boroughs the dates are usually the second weekend in September. For details of the buildings that will be open, write to Heritage Open Day, Civic Trust, 17 Carlton House Terrace, London SW1Y 5AW, enclosing six second class stamps.

London Open House
0181-341 1371   Hotline 0891-600061
Heritage Open Day (see previous entry) is a national event. The London equivalent takes place a week later (the third weekend in September). There are also walks, exhibitions and lectures. For details, look for leaflets in galleries around town or, for a comprehensive booklet, send an SAE with 39p in stamps on it and £1 in stamps inside, a couple of months in advance to: London Open House, West Hill House, 6 Swains Lane, London N6 6QU.

London Wildlife Trust N1
80 York Way   0171-278 6612
The Trust's aim is to sustain and enhance London's wildlife habitats and it manages 57 nature reserves – a free map of locations is available. Each year, more than 600 free indoor and outdoor events are organised – from bat walks to wildflower talks. You can call the number given to obtain information packs and factsheets, as well as details of events.

Attractions all round London

Bus tours
If, as we assume, you already have a Travelcard, you can explore London from the best possible vantage point – the upper platform of a double-decker bus – at no cost. This form of tour has the virtue you can hop on and hop off to your heart's content. If you find there are so many things to do you don't have time to finish your planned circuit, it hardly matters.

With one of London Transport's free bus guides, you can plan your own tour, but there are two routes which are particularly suitable for a general orientation.

The number 11 takes you on a great East-West tour of London and includes many of the major sights. Start your trip at the stop in Chelsea's fashionable King's Road and ride through Victoria to Westminster Abbey. This would be a good place to break the journey and to walk a short way: through Parliament Square, and down Whitehall to look at 10 Downing Street and the Cenotaph. Hop back on the bus at Trafalgar Square – where you find Nelson's Column and the National Gallery (see also), travel down the Strand and Fleet Street and end at St Paul's Cathedral.

The number 15 (pick it up at Paddington, Edgware Road, Oxford Street or Regent Street) shares the Trafalgar Square to St Paul's section with the number 11 (so you can change at any point between the two). However, the former continues into the City enabling you to see the Monument, Tower Bridge and the Tower of London. Travel on this route on a Sunday morning and you might press on to Aldgate, for Petticoat Lane market.

On a Saturday, consider venturing into Notting Hill on the number 12 or 94 (from Regent Street or Oxford Street). This is one of the nicest parts of inner London for a walk, but on Saturday the special attraction is the Portobello Road market.

Courts
If you've half a day to kill you might find it interesting, and perhaps amusing, to spend it in court. There are three types of court which will be within easy reach of most parts of London – magistrates, crown and county courts.

All human life passes through London's magistrates courts, where the highest and the lowest appear to explain why they have (or have not) committed minor criminal offences, from drunkenness to speeding.

Londonwide information

Sometimes it will be pretty humdrum stuff (if not without human interest). If you hit lucky, however, you may experience a real trial, probably not lasting more than a day, where the question "did he (or she) do it?" is of more than academic interest, especially to the person in the dock.

In the Crown courts, the more serious crimes – all the way up to murder – are tried by a judge and jury. The disadvantage for the casual visitor is that most trials go on for several days, so inevitably you will see only a fraction of the proceedings. By far the most interesting theatre is to be found when a witness (especially the defendant) is being cross-examined by the opposing side's bewigged counsel. The Old Bailey (see The City) is London's senior Crown court.

County Courts resolve civil disputes (such as claims for damages, perhaps arising from a motor accident, or for unpaid money owed). Again, cross-examination is generally by far the most gripping part of a trial. The most important civil trials take place at the Royal Courts of Justice (see The City).

To find the address of your local court, consult the telephone directory. Courts generally sit between 10.00 and 16.30. Children under 16 are not usually admitted into the public galleries.

Fire stations
It may be possible to organise a visit to your local fire brigade. Write to the Commander at your nearest station.

Events

Regular events

The following ceremonial events happen all through
the year.

Ceremony of the Keys
Tower of London, EC3   0171-709 0765
*In accordance with seven centuries of tradition, the Tower of
London (home, of course, to the Crown Jewels) is secured for
the night with a brief ceremony. Anyone can apply for a ticket
to attend, but you need to do so in writing (Ceremony of the
Keys, HM Tower of London, London EC3N 4AB) and give at
least two months' notice. / Times: nightly at 21.30; Tube: Tower Hill.*

Changing the Guard (Buckingham Palace)
Buckingham Palace, SW1
*The changing of the sentries at Buckingham Palace is famous
around the world. The new guard leaves Wellington Barracks
three minutes before the change, and, preceded by a band,
marches down Birdcage Walk to the palace. The ceremony
itself lasts 40 minutes, and takes place inside the railings of
the palace. The event is subject to cancellation in very bad
weather or during state visits. / Times: Apr-Oct, daily, 11.30; Nov-Mar,
every other day; Tube: Green Park.*

Changing the Guard (Horse Guards)
Horse Guards Parade, SW1
*In a daily burst of pageantry, a mounted guard leaves
Hyde Park Barracks at 10.28 (Sun 09.28) and proceeds,
via Hyde Park Corner and Constitution Hill to arrive at
Horse Guards Parade at 11.00 (Sun 10.00), where the guard
is changed. The splendidly attired mounted guardsmen
making their way through Hyde Park offers one of London's
most romantic sights. / Times: daily 11.00, Sun 10.00; Tube: Hyde Park
Corner, St James's Park.*

Gun Salutes
*One of the most striking sights in London is the gun salutes
which hail royal and state events. These take place in Green
or Hyde Parks (12.00) and at the Tower of London (13.00)
on the following dates (or, if a Sunday, the following day):
6 February (Accession Day); 21 April (the Queen's birthday);
2 June (Coronation Day); 10 June (the Duke of Edinburgh's
birthday); and 4 August (the Queen Mother's birthday).
Salutes also mark state visits (usually in May and October),
Trooping the Colour (June) and the State Opening of
Parliament (October or November). Details of these and other
events in the Royal Parks are given in the Summer
Entertainment Programme available with an A5 SAE from
the Old Police House, Hyde Park, London W2 2UH
(0171-298 2000). / Tube: Hyde Park Corner, Tower Hill.*

Annual diary

Barely a month goes by in London without some great event happening, which can provide a good focus for a day out, especially with children in tow. The major events which happen on an annual basis are as follows.

January _____

London Parade
The New Year starts with a bang, in the form of a relatively new, American-style family event on the first day of the year. Hundreds of thousands of people turn out to see the big parade, with 6,000 majorettes (flown in from the US), floats and dance displays. It starts from Parliament Square at noon and the final band reaches Berkeley Square in Mayfair around 14.45. The procession includes horse-drawn carriages in which ride the mayors of Westminster and of all the London boroughs (but not, of course, the fiercely independent City).
/ Tube: Westminster, St James's, Green Park.

Chinese New Year
In late January or early February, Chinatown celebrates the Chinese New Year with noisy, colourful parades (including the famous papier mâché dragons), which last most of the day. The whole area (around Gerrard Street W1) is brightly decorated for the event. / Tube: Leicester Square.

February _____

Shrove Tuesday Pancake Races
Covent Garden, WC2 and Spitalfields Market, E1
Shrove Tuesday ("Pancake Day") sees traditional races between pancake-tossing relay-teams at Covent Garden (check time) and Spitalfields (12.30) Markets.
/ Tube: Covent Garden, Leicester Square/Liverpool St.

Events

Head of the River Race
0181-940 2219

The Oxford and Cambridge Boat Race may be more famous, but, for the casual observer, the Head of the River race, rowed on a Saturday in March from Mortlake to Putney, may be more interesting to watch. The sheer number of crews (usually over 400) means that the colourful procession of eight-oared boats (which are set off ten seconds apart) takes well over an hour. Being a timed race, it does have the disadvantage that no-one knows who has won until it's all over. Best vantage points are as for the Boat Race (below), but those in the know go to Chiswick Bridge to watch the pre-race marshalling of hundreds of boats in a confined stretch of the river. / Tube: Putney Bridge.

Kite Festival
Blackheath, SE3

Easter Sunday and Monday see London's leading kite festival – a great spectacle whether you're interested in kite-flying or not. (Devotees might like to note there are also two smaller events in the summer – here and in Hackney Marshes.) / Rail: Blackheath.

London Marathon
0171-620 4117

The London Marathon, first run in 1981, has grown into a huge event which attracts more than 30,000 participants and over a half a million spectators. Its sheer scale and spectacle makes it a good family day out. Over half of the runners are taking part for charity (and collectively raise over £10 million). Many compete in costume, and you may see some famous faces. The course of just over 26 miles begins (around 09.00) on Blackheath and ends (having taken a circuitous route) outside Buckingham Palace. The leaders take a little over a couple of hours to complete the course, but the stragglers ensure it's practically an all-day event.

Oxford and Cambridge Boat Race

It may be an arcane and thoroughly English way of spending an afternoon, but the world's most famous boat-race, first rowed on the Thames in 1849, still exercises an extraordinary grip on the popular imagination, and tens of thousands of people turn out every year to snatch a passing glimpse of an 18-minute race which, from a practical point of view, is much better watched on television. The best vantage points for the four-mile race from Putney to Mortlake are generally held to be at the half-way point (Hammersmith) or at the finish – but you don't get much of a view anywhere and the real point is not really the race but the atmosphere. Take a picnic – and, if you want to know who's won, a radio. / Tube: Putney Bridge.

Canalway Cavalcade
Pool of Little Venice, Paddington, W9   0181-674 2787
*Crafts of all types, music, morris dancing, boat trips and
waterway-related trade and craft stalls make this annual
boat rally, organised by the Inland Waterways Association,
a lively, colourful event with plenty to see for all the family.
A night-time highlight is the illuminated boat procession which
takes place on the Sunday evening. / Times: May Day Bank Hol
weekend, 10.00-18.00 & Sun eve; Tube: Warwick Avenue.*

Coin Street Festival SE1
Gabriel's Wharf, SE1   0171-401 3610
*Popular and growing all-free event that runs from
mid-June to September, and which celebrates the many
cultures and interest of the people who live or work in, or visit
the capital. Highlights are live music and street performances,
and there are many activities for children, including
workshops and competitions. Almost every weekend there is a
day of events, usually around a particular theme – call for a
leaflet. / Tube: Waterloo, Blackfriars, (from October '98 Southwark).*

Covent Garden Festival
67 Long Acre, Covent Garden, WC2   0171-405 7555
*During the Covent Garden festival, a stage is put up at the
west end of the Piazza and a range of opera and musical
works is performed. Some of the events are free. Call for a
festival brochure. / Tube: Covent Garden, Leicester Square.*

Highbury Festival of Music and the Arts
Highbury Fields, N5   0171-477 3853,
(Islington Arts & Heritage Department)
*Most of the musical events of this annual festival, which takes
place during the first two weeks in May, carry an entry fee.
However, Bank Holiday Monday sees Jazz on the Fields – a
day-long family jazz extravaganza. There are also exhibitions
of art (all free) for the duration of the festival in Islington
galleries and at Christ Church, Highbury, the focus of the
Festival. Call the number given for details of events.
/ Tube: Highbury & Islington.*

Museums Week
*During one week in May (usually starting on the third
Saturday) around 850 museums in the capital and across
the country – including many of the free institutions listed
in this book – put on special events. Full details appear in*
Radio Times, *or you can check out the web-site at*
http://www.museumsweek.co.uk.

Events

May Fayre and Puppet Festival
St Paul's Church and Gardens, WC2   0171-375 0441
*All-day event, celebrating the art of puppetry with Punch and
Judy professors from all over the country. Parade from 10.30
and Church service in St Paul's Church from 11.30.*
/ Tube: Covent Garden, Leicester Square.

June

Croydon Jazz Festival *
0181-760 5400 ext 1037
*Previously called Croydon Jazz Week, and known for its trad
jazz, this borough-wide festival now concentrates on the
modern and latin varieties. It takes place during the first
two weeks of June. Most of the free events take place at
lunchtime. / Rail: Croydon.*

Dulwich Country Fayre
Dulwich Park, College Rd, SE22   0171-525 3735
*The Fayre comprises five areas of interest: the Equine; Home
and Garden; Canine (with demonstrations from working dogs
including those of the Metropolitan Police); Motors and the
Entertainments (including magic and circus skills workshops
and games). There are also trade stands, a cycle circuit and a
bandstand. / Times: Sat & Sun 11.00-18.00; Rail: North or West Dulwich.*

Spitalfields Festival
Christ Church, Commercial St, E1
Hotline: 0171-377 1362
*Hawksmoor's imposing Christ Church is the setting for a
classical music festival. Every June there is a varied
programme of lunchtime and evening concerts with music
from c15-c20. Many events are free but there may be a
retiring collection. Complementary exhibitions and a fringe
festival take place in the same month. The latter event
includes arts events, comedy and circus performance
(0171-375 0441). / Tube: Shoreditch, Liverpool Street.*

Stoke Newington Midsummer Festival
Box Office, c/o Stoke newington Library Foyer,
Stoke Newington Church St, N16   0181-442 5255
*This week-long arts festival showcases Hackney-based artists,
performers and musicians. Many events, including poetry
readings, walks and listening to the dawn chorus, are free.
Visual art includes installations and photographic exhibitions
and take place in unusual places including Abney Park
Cemetery (see also). / Rail: Stoke Newington or 73 bus.*

Tierra Latino
Kennington Park, SE11
0171-228 1090, or 0181-674 3314
*Exuberan family event on second weekend in June with
non-stop Latin American music, live bands and dancing. There
is also a funfair and stalls selling ethnic food. / Tube: Oval.*

Trooping the Colour
0171-930 4466

A Saturday in early June sees the celebration of the Queen's Official Birthday, when she inspects an elaborate military display at Horse Guards Parade SW1. At 13.00, after her return to Buckingham Palace, there is an RAF fly-past down the Mall.

There is a charge to attend the event itself (although, of course, you can watch the procession down the Mall), but tickets for the first rehearsal, The Major General's Review, (two or three Saturdays before) are free, and (as for the main event itself) are allocated by ballot. Apply in January or February, with an SAE, to Brigade Major (Trooping the Colour), Headquarters, Household Division, Horse Guards, Whitehall London SW1A 2AX. / Tube: St James's Park.

Flower Festival
The Piazza, Covent Garden, WC2   0171-836 9136
Taking place in the last week of June in this former fruit and veg market, the Festival presents innovative and contemporary flower displays and garden installations combined with theatrical productions and promotions – it's aimed particularly at the urban gardener. The main attraction is the performance garden, a large-scale installation in front of St Paul's Church offering a platform for street theatre, opera, music and dance. / Tube: Covent Garden, Leicester Square.

*June/July*_____

City of London Festival
City Festival Box Office, St Paul's Churchyard, London EC4M 8BU   0171-377 0540
In late June/early July the City enjoys an explosion of music. If you're looking for free events, seek out the Fringe brochure – there's not much that's alternative about it, but it's where most of the no-charge events are listed. In it, you will find, on any one weekday, up to half a dozen lunchtime concerts in churches – all without charge, though contributions to the retiring collection will be welcome.

The Festival's Opening Service (morning) is effectively a sung eucharist followed by a free choral concert in the magnificent setting of St Paul's. There is almost invariably a charge for the evening events.

Events

Henley Royal Regatta
01491-572153

Henley, established in 1839, is the world's oldest major rowing regatta. It takes place in late June/early July (the final Sunday is always the 27th Sunday of the year). Even if you've never been in a rowing boat in your life, and even if you don't know anyone who is a member of one of the enclosures, it's still one of the most enjoyable events of "the Season"; it manages, to an extraordinary extent, to maintain something of the atmosphere of an Edwardian garden party. Take a picnic, arrive early, and find a good viewpoint along the towpath. All but the last third of a mile or so of the course is open to the public, and at many points you can hear the commentary. The event lasts from Wednesday to Sunday — it's much less crowded on the weekdays. / Rail: Henley.

July

Hillingdon Borough Carnival
Hayes, Middx   01895-250648   off map

Every year the second weekend in July sees the streets of Hayes erupt with floats and crowds. Up to 20 floats, followed by marching bands, lead the way from Pump Lane at 12.30, to Barra Hall Park, by 14.00. Here there is a fun fair, Punch and Judy shows, clowns, stalls, pony rides, live music and stilt-walking. / Rail: Hayes.

Hackney Show
Hackney Downs, Downs Rd, E5   0171-762 6830

All the events and activities at this family fun day are free (except the funfair). Enjoy live music on one of several stages, or watch dance troupes perform. Look out for stalls, an international food village, clowns, jugglers and stilt walkers. A children's area and a film tent showing films suitable for all the family mean no matter your age or the weather everyone will enjoy him- or herself. / Times: 1st Sat in July, 12.00-20.00; Rail: Hackney Central.

Swan Upping
0171-236 1863

All the swans on the Thames between London Bridge and Henley belong to the Queen, or one of two of the City Livery Companies: the Dyers or the Vintners. This cosy three-way arrangement has been in place since 1510

Each year, it is necessary to mark the cygnets to show to whom they belong (which depends, of course, on who owns their parents). This task is carried out every July by a procession of six "Thames Skiffs" (rowed by colourfully uniformed oarsmen), which takes a week to progress from Sunbury to Sonning. Traditionally, swans were marked by nicking their beaks, but they are now (from 1997) ringed instead – this is, of course, still known as "nicking". If you want to know when and where you can witness this extraordinary ritual call the Vintners on the number given.

Greenwich Festival *
0181-305 1818, festival hotline 0181-853 4444 (brochures/bookings)
London's principal multi-arts extravaganza now spans both banks of the Thames, and, as from 1997, moves to July. Many of the attractions are free and include opening and closing night pyrotechnics, open-air jazz performances and dance in the squares and colonnades of the Royal Naval College. For details, you an visit the web-site at http://www.festival.org. / Rail: Greenwich, Woolwich (DLR).

August _____

Ealing Jazz Festival
0181-758 5743
After 13 years in existence, the "friendly festival" claims to be the largest free jazz festival in Britain. All bands are led by local musicians. There are performances at lunchtimes and in the evening. Play- and games-areas for children are somtimes provided. / Tube: Ealing Broadway.

Notting Hill Carnival
The August Bank holiday sees the largest street party in Europe – a million people attending a noisy celebration of Afro-Caribbean culture. The events, centred around the northern parts of the Portobello Road, take place over the Sunday and the Monday, with the second day seeing the carnival procession proper.

It's certainly impressive in its sheer scale and vitality, but this may make it rather daunting to some people. All the commonsense rules of attending such a large and crowded occasion apply – don't drive to it, keep hold of children, and carry as little money as possible. All the festivities happen during the day and it's best not to hang around in the evening. / Tube: Notting Hill Gate, Ladbroke Grove.

Events

Walpole Festival, Ealing
0181-758 5743   1–2A
*In the lead-up to the summer festival at Walpole Park, a
roadshow takes place in several of the borough's other parks.
Many of the events are free and include shows and activities
for children. Entertainments include arena displays, theatrical
performances and sports events. In the evenings, shows – for
which there may be a charge or donations sought – might
include comedy, religious and rhythm 'n' blues. The festival is
immediately followed by the Ealing Jazz Festival (see also).*
/ Tube: Ealing Broadway.

September

Covent Garden Festival of Street Theatre
Covent Garden, WC2   0171-836 9136
*For two weeks, Covent Garden Market celebrates street
theatre, with a range of high quality acts throughout the day.*
/ Tube: Covent Garden, Leicester Square.

Great River Race
c/o Stuart Wolff 0181-398 9057
*Celebrating its tenth birthday in 1997, this ever more popular
event has all the ingredients of a Great British Success Story.
For a start, the idea behind it is completely – inspiringly –
batty. Take more than 250 oared boats (rule: no racing-boats
allowed), devise a handicapping system (which allows some
boats to start 100 minutes before others) and set them off
(down a tidal river) on a 22-mile journey from Ham House in
Richmond to Island Gardens on the Isle of Dogs. The event
attracts every type of boat (from Chinese dragon boats to
Hawaiian war canoes) and rowers and paddlers of all ages
and of every degree of seriousness from all over the world.
It's a wonderful spectacle, and one which can be viewed
from any London bank of the Thames (though the greatest
excitement is, of course, at the start and the finish
(from around noon). / Tube: choice of 12 between Richmond and
Island Gardens (DLR).*

National Trust Free Entry Day
*There's generally a charge to enter National Trust properties
(except for members), but on one day a year many properties
are open free of charge. Needless to say, if you value
tranquillity, this is probably not the best time to go. The Trust
does not generally advertise the date – for fear of attracting
crowds of people who can perfectly well afford to pay – so
you'll have to keep your ear to the ground.*

Raising of the Thames Barrier
Unity Way, SE18   0181-854 1373
Canute was wrong – you can hold back the tide, but only by spending half a billion pounds on a great river barrier, designed to protect central London from the ever-growing risk of flooding. The Thames Barrier (see also) is a miracle of modern engineering (completed in 1982). Once a year (usually in September or October) there is an all-day test and the massive steel gates are either raised (six) or dropped (four) against the high tide. There are also tests each month, but these take place as early in the morning as tides permit and (because it involves closing a working river) for as short a period as possible. Call the Visitor Centre on the number above for details. / Rail: Charlton; Café.

Thamesday
0171-620 0544
From Frost Fairs to GLC Thames Days. the London's river has long been a natural focal point for pageantry and celebrations. It is hoped that, in the area between the Pool of London and London Bridge, it will be again from 1999. Intervening years will be marked with smaller-scale events. / Tube: Waterloo, Westminster.

October _____

Punch and Judy Festival
Covent Garden, WC2   0171-836 9136
The first Sunday of October sees a plethora of Punch and Judy shows and their continental equivalents – Polichinelle (France), Kasper (Germany) and Pulcinella (Italy).
/ Tube: Covent Garden, Leicester Square.

State Opening of Parliament
If you want to see the Queen wearing a crown and riding in a gilded coach, the only annual opportunity to do so is the State Opening of Parliament (usually in October). Her Majesty rides from Buckingham Palace to Westminster to deliver the Queen's Speech (which sets out the Government's legislative plans for the forthcoming year, and is, in fact, written by the Prime Minister) and then returns to her palace. There are accompanying gun salutes at Green Park and the Tower of London. As an event, it's not hugely well attended and offers possibly the best royal-watching opportunity of the year.
/ Tube: Westminster.

Events

Fireworks Night

The annual remembrance of the failure of the Gunpowder plot (to blow up monarch, lords and commoners assembled at Westminster) is celebrated with bonfire and firework parties of all sizes all over London. Parties take place on November 5 and, if it falls mid-week, the weekends before and after. The larger events – Battersea Park, for example – are widely advertised on posters and in local newspapers.

Lord Mayor's Show

The Lord Mayor's Show has taken place – plague permitting – in some form in most years since 1215. It celebrates the annual presentation of the new Lord Mayor of London to the Queen's Justices. This formerly took place at Westminster but now involves a rather shorter journey to the Royal Courts of Justice in the Strand. The show takes place on the second Saturday of November. It begins at the Guildhall at 11.00 and its heart is a 1 1/2 mile procession which includes 60 floats, 20 bands and about 5,000 people. The centrepiece of the procession is the Lord Mayor's gilded, c18 coach (housed for the rest of the year in the Museum of London, see also), pulled by six shire horses. This is a great traditional Londoners' outing – a whole day's entertainment is provided, ending with a firework display over the Thames - and about a quarter of a million people attend annually. Many City attractions, which are generally closed at the weekends, open on the day of the show. / Tube: Bank.

RAC London to Brighton Veteran Car Run

Saturday 14 November 1896 was a great day in the history of British motoring – for the first time it was legal to proceed at more than 4mph and without being preceded by a man with a red flag. Ever since (war years excepted) horseless carriages have taken part in an annual celebration of automobile 'emancipation'. The Run – it is NOT a race – takes place on the first Sunday in November, leaving Hyde Park at 07.30, and progressing via Westminster (07.35) and Lambeth Town Hall (07.45) to Brighton, where the front-runners arrive around 10.30. Only cars built before 1905 are eligible to take part, and competitors come from all over the world. More than a million people watch the run each year. / Tube: Hyde Park Corner.

Remembrance Sunday
Whitehall, SW1
The Sunday nearest 11 November sees the most sober large-scale event of the year. Just after 11.00, the Queen and representatives of the government and the Commonwealth lay wreaths of Flanders poppies at the Cenotaph to commemorate those who gave their lives in war. After the short service, the tone becomes a little lighter as the veterans march past. / Tube: Embankment, Charing Cross, Westminster.

Christmas Parade
An American-style parade – with 2,000 participants including dancers, clowns, marching bands and floats that takes place from Berkeley Square, Oxford and Regent Streets to Piccadilly Circus – which takes place on one Sunday in late November.
/ Tube: Oxford Circus, Piccadilly Circus, Bond Street.

December _____

Christmas lights
The heartland of London's shopping – Oxford Street, Regent Street and, in a rather more subdued way, Bond Street – generally puts on a reasonable show with its Christmas lights. The illuminations are given a celebrity 'switch on' in November and they are there to be admired until Twelfth Night. An evening visit to this part of town around this time also permits some vigorous window-shopping at Selfridges and the other stores of Oxford Street, and at Hamleys and Liberty on Regent Street. Simpson and Fortnum & Mason on Piccadilly usually put on a pretty good display as well. Do note that, in the run-up to Christmas, the whole of the centre of the West End can be surprisingly crowded well after the shops have closed. / Tube: Marble Arch, Oxford Circus, Bond Street, Piccadilly Circus.

Christmas tree
Trafalgar Square, WC2
The great Christmas tree in Trafalgar Square, decorated with bright white lamps, is an annual gift from the citizens of Oslo to the people of London. There are regular carol concerts around the tree. / Tube: Charing Cross.

New Year's Eve
Trafalgar Square, WC2
Packing yourself into Trafalgar Square is traditionally the way to see in the New Year in London. Those who do not like crowds should stay away, and even those who do should think twice – as midnight approaches the drunken crush can be unbearable and it can be so crowded as to be impossible to get into the Square itself. Getting home is, unusually, free of charge as London Transport operates its (usually sponsored) offer of free transport throughout the capital, with the tubes running well past midnight. / Tube: Charing Cross.

Entertainments

Entertainments

Radio & TV
audience participation

London's position as a great centre of music and broadcasting means there's a huge amount of entertainment of almost every kind – from classical concerts to game-shows. And it's just there for the asking, as being a member of the studio audience at such events is almost invariably free.

Below, we give the details of the organisations which produce recitals, concerts and TV and radio programmes. It's worth remembering that, even for radio and TV, it's surprising what you may be able to pick up at short notice.

Radio

BBC
Radio Ticket Unit, BBC, London W1A 4WW
Recorded information 0171-765 5858
Enquiries 0171-765 5243
Radio shows tend to be scheduled only about six weeks ahead of broadcasting, so audience tickets are often available at short notice. The recorded information service tells you what's on offer (it's on CEEFAX, too) and enables you to leave your ticket request. or you can get information by post.

For a one-off query send an SAE, but they will, on request, put your name on a mailing list and you will be kept up to date with what's available. There's something for almost all tastes, from classical concerts, via easy listening and discussions, to quiz programmes.

Radio shows are mainly recorded at the following venues: the BBC Radio Theatre at Broadcasting House W1; the Hippodrome, North End Road NW11; and the Maida Vale Studios, Delaware Road W9.

Television

BBC
Audience Services, Room 301, Design Building, Television Centre London W12 7RJ   0181-576 1227
There's a huge choice of comedies, variety shows, quiz programmes and debates you can go and watch being recorded during the afternoon and evening. First, ring to check the BBC makes the programme you want to see (ie that it is not done by a separate production company - such as Have I Got News For You, which is made by Hat Trick Productions, see also) and that there is a series coming up. Then send an SAE to Audience Services who will send you

information about what's currently on offer. People drop out at short notice and it is worth trying even for shows happening in the near future. Singles and parties are welcome and this is an ideal outing for all ages that costs no more than the coach hire. Children aged under 14 are not generally admitted. Further information is also available at http://www.bbc.co.uk/tventertainment/tickets.html (and you can send messages via e-mail to tv.ticket.unit@bbc.co.uk).

Channel 5

Channel 5 Duty Office, PO Box 55,
Nottingham NG1 5HE   0345-050505
Companies making programmes for the new station may advertise for audience members, perhaps in Time Out. *Channel 5 does not have a mailing list but you can keep up-to-date with what's available via the Duty Office.*

ITV

Many of the most popular independent TV shows, are filmed at the London TV Centre on the South Bank. However, the in-house audience unit has now closed and, as we went to press, it was not clear what system would replace the current set-up – you could start by calling the main switchboard number (0171-620 1620).

Many ITV (and also now some BBC) programmes are made by relatively small, independent production companies (see also Hat Trick Productions) and some have a policy of advertising for audience participants when (and only when) they want to recruit. Keep an eye on the media – Time Out *and* Private Eye *are favoured – especially in the autumn.*

Inspired PR of 9 Crondal Place, Edgbaston, Birmingham B15 2LB (0121-440 1633) specialises in finding audiences and maintains a mailing list. It is employed by some of the smaller, independent TV production companies and often looks for people in the London area. Send an SAE for details of forthcoming shows.

If you really want to see a particular programme, however, there's no substitute for tracking down the production company concerned and asking how it allocates tickets.

Hat Trick Productions
0171-287 1598, Mon–Fri (ticketline)
0171-434 2451 ext 7005 (recorded information)
Most famous for Have I Got News for You, *this independent company also does* Drop the Dead Donkey, *and* Whose Line is it Anyway? *There's no mailing list and it seems regulars call the ticketline number every six weeks to check availability. You need to ring several months in advance to stand a chance of getting tickets for your favourite show – for the most popular, tickets go on the day they become available. Generally, the minimum age is 15. Recording is at the LWT Studios on the South Bank.*

Music

City music
There is music in one of the many churches of the City almost every lunchtime – almost all concerts begin between 13.00 and 13.15 and generally last no more than an hour. A useful monthly publication, City Events, *available from the City of London Information Centre by St Paul's, gives advance details. Alternatively, if you arrive at the centre by 12.40 you should have time to locate the concert of your choice and walk to the appropriate church.*

The top time of year for music is during the City of London Festival (see also) in late June/early July.

The Corporation of London also presents a series of band concerts through the summer at four locations (Finsbury Circus, Tower Place, Royal Exchange Forecourt and St Paul's Cathedral Steps) from 12.00 to 14.00 on Wednesdays and Thursdays from June to September – you can get a leaflet from the Information Centre.

Events in the Royal Parks
Most of the Royal Parks (Hyde, Regent's, St James's, Green, Greenwich and Richmond, and Kensington Gardens) have music, and other events, on a regular basis. It's well worth sending an A5 SAE to Old Police House, Hyde Park, London W2 2UH (0171-298 2000), asking for a Summer Entertainment Programme. *Events of interest to adults include theatrical and operatic productions, dancing demonstrations and guided nature and gardening tours of the parks. For children there are circus acts and puppet shows.*

Guildhall School of Music and Drama *
Barbican, Silk St, EC2   0171-382 7218   5–1C
Opera, jazz, ensemble, contemporary music... Events, most of which are free, take place at the School, at the Barbican, and elsewhere, lunchtimes and evenings. Call for the termly programme which gives full details. / Tube: Moorgate, Barbican.

Music colleges

London boasts some of the finest music colleges in the world and, to those who enjoy classical music they represent an extremely fertile source of free entertainment.

All the schools listed give three or four concerts or recitals a week during their term times. The most popular performances tend to be the larger ones – those with symphony orchestras or works with a large chorus – of which there may be five or so in a term at a given school.

Royal Academy of Music

Marylebone Rd, NW1   0171-873 7300   2–1A
Details of the around ten free events, mostly unticketed, that take place every week are listed in the termly Diary of Events *available from the box office on the number given.*
/ Tube: Baker Street; Café.

Royal College of Music

Prince Consort Rd, SW7
0171-589 3643, ext 4380   3–1B
Most of the performances are given at the college, just behind the Royal Albert Hall, although a number are held at other venues around the capital. For example, at 13.10 on Fridays during term time, a concert is given at the imposing church of St Mary Abbots in the centre of Kensington (tube: High Street Kensington). / Tube: (College) South Kensington.

Shell LSO Music Scholarship Final

Barbican Concert Hall, Silk St, EC2   0171-638 8891
The £6,000 Shell LSO Music Scholarship is one of the most prestigious prizes available to young musicians. The competition final is held in late June/early July each year and involves the LSO performing selected movements with the four competitors. It's a very enjoyable event if you prefer listening to classical music in a very informal atmosphere. Tickets are allocated on a first come, first served basis by the Barbican Box Office – contact the number given, or for more information call the LSO Scholarship Administrator on 0171-588 1116. / Tube: Barbican, Moorgate.

Trinity College of Music

11 Mandeville Place, W1   0171-935 5773 ext 242   2–1A
Most concerts and recitals take place around 13.00 in the Barbirolli Lecture Hall or in the nearby Hinde Street church. Free Diary of Events *from the number given. / Tube: Bond Street.*

Other venues

Most of the major arts centres offer free foyer music (often of very high quality) on a regular basis – details are given under the entries for the respective venues. See the Royal Festival Hall (South) and the Royal National Theatre (South), the Barbican (The City). Other places listed which offer regular free music are Westminster Abbey (Central) and St Mary Abbots (West).

Central London

Introduction

The fact that Central London is at the ceremonial and governmental heart of Britain – comprising as it does the **Houses of Parliament**, **Westminster Abbey**, **Buckingham Palace** and 10 Downing Street – provides an almost unequalled range of famous historic attractions. The Abbey and, with planning, Parliament can be visited.

Art and antiquities is another major theme of an area which contains some of the most significant museums and art galleries in the world. In the mega-league are the **British Museum** and the **Tate** and **National Galleries**. There are, however, also smaller attractions with first-rate collections – among these, the **Wallace Collection** and **Sir John Soane's Museum** stand out.

In addition, the commercial art world provides a huge and ever-changing selection of pictures and objects to view, and the institutions which deal in them have their own special interest and charm. A visit to one of the great auctioneers, such as **Sotheby's** and **Christie's** combines art with theatre. For a guide to the commercial galleries see *Galleries* on page 13.

The area is a window-shopper's paradise, containing as it does most of the UK's top shops. These range from **Harrods** and **Fortnum & Mason** at the larger end of the scale to the opulent boutiques of **Old Bond Street**, and the charming, small shops in the Regency **Burlington Arcade**. Almost all the very central areas have sufficient character to justify just strolling around, but **Covent Garden** would probably be on most lists and boasts outdoor entertainers and a variety of festivals year-round.

With children, this is a rather tiring area. There are the sights of course – one can add **Trafalgar Square** and **Eros** to those already mentioned – and there is also the possibility of a trip to **Hamleys**, the toy shop. Leaving this aside, the top attractions for families are probably **St James's Park** – which is pretty and interesting enough to provide something for everyone – and Bloomsbury's **Coram's Fields**, a great amenity for kids.

London Tourist Board SW1
Victoria Station   2–4B
The main outlet of the tourist board is in front of Victoria Station. (See entry on page 11) / Tube: Victoria.

Indoor attractions

Alfred Dunhill SW1
48 Jermyn St   0171-290 8600   2–3B
Jermyn Street, London's most discreet shopping thoroughfare, boasts the headquarters of one of the great success stories of international luxury branded goods. The Alfred Dunhill Museum (now in the basement of the recently refurbished shop) houses examples of motoring accessories, jewellery, watches, handbags and smoking items manufactured by the company over the last century. Give 48 hours notice and you can arrange a guided tour. / Times: Mon-Sat 09.30 (Sat 10.00)-18.00; Tube: Green Park, Piccadilly Circus.

Architectural Association WC1
34-36 Bedford Square   0171-636 0974   2–1C
For anyone with an interest in architecture, the Association offers a rich and varied programme of afternoon and evening lectures. There are also usually three exhibitions on single projects by contemporary architects running concurrently.
/ Times: Mon-Fri 10.00-19.00, Sat 10.00-15.00; Tube: Tottenham Court Road.

Architecture Centre, Royal Institute of British Architects (RIBA) W1
66 Portland Place   0171-631 0460   2–1B
The Architecture Centre is an international showcase for today and the future, and focuses on awards and competitions. However, it also shows some off-the-wall exhibitions and hosts a film festival. (See also Heinz Gallery, RIBA.) / Times: Mon, Wed, Fri & Sat 08.00-18.00; Tue & Thu 08.00-21.00; Tube: Oxford Circus, Great Portland Street, Regents Park; Café.

Architecture Foundation SW1
The Economist Building, 30 Bury St
0171-839 9389   2–3B
This relatively recently established body is "dedicated to the display and discussion of contemporary architecture and the built environment in a way that appeals to the public". In addition to the exhibition programme it holds a series of forums on architectural and urban planning questions to which the public is invited. / Times: Tue-Sun 12.00-18.00, or by appointment; Tube: Green Park.

Ben Uri Art Society NW1
Ort House, 126 Albert St   0171-482 1234
The Society moved to temporary accommodation in spring 1997 but has no exhibition space of its own. Its works will be displayed in galleries around town – contact the Society for details of when, what and where! The collection includes more than 800 works by Jewish artists including Bomberg, Auerbach, Epstein and Kitaj. Further information is also available at http://www.ort.org/benuri/ (or you can e-mail the Society at benuri@ort.org).

BOC Museum WC1

Association of Anaesthetists of Great Britain and Ireland,
9 Bedford Square 0171-631 1650 2–1C
In the mid '20s, a medical instrument maker, Charles King, started to collect anaesthetic apparatus. These items were donated to the Association in the '50s and became the nucleus of the museum which is now home to one of the largest collections of this type in the world. The Association does not have space to display all its 5,000 items – instead it puts on an annual exhibition on a specific topic. / Times: by telephone appointment with the Administration Manager; Tube: Goodge Street, Tottenham Court Road.

British Dental Association Museum W1

64 Wimpole St 0171-935 0875 2–1B
*The Association's extensive museum covers the history of British dentistry since the c18 and features equipment, furniture, re-created surgeries and cartoon prints.
/ Times: by appointment Mon-Fri 10.00-16.00; Tube: Regent's Park, Bond Street.*

British Museum WC1

Great Russell St 0171-636 1555 2–1C
*Six million visitors a year can't be wrong – this august neo-classical building (Robert Smirke, 1823–52) is London's leading attraction – free or otherwise. It does, after all, house what is arguably the world's greatest collection of antiquities. Particular strengths include Egyptian artefacts, coins and medals, the collections relating to Greek and Roman civilisation (especially, of course, the marbles from the Parthenon), clocks, and prints and drawings. No-one could possibly take in the whole museum in a day – just to pass by all the exhibits would apparently require a walk of some 2 1/2 miles – so it's probably worth deciding on a section of particular interest and trying to make sense of that. From Tuesday to Saturday, the museum's experts give gallery talks at 11.30 and lectures at 13.15. There are many interesting temporary exhibitions (mostly free), regular talks and films, and even occasional art workshops for children.
/ Times: Mon-Sat 10.00-17.00, Sun 14.30-18.00; Tube: Russell Square, Tottenham Court Road, Holborn.*

Burlington Arcade W1

Between Piccadilly and Burlington Gardens 2–2B
This Regency shopping arcade is perhaps the most timeless place in London for window-shopping. Top-hatted beadles maintain standards – no running, no singing, no carrying large parcels etc – leaving you in perfect serenity to survey the displays in the windows of the small, elegant shops, many of which still sell hand-made luxury goods. / Times: Mon-Sat 09.00-17.30; Tube: Green Park, Piccadilly Circus.

Christie's SW1
8 King St   0171-839 9060   2–3B

The two great international auction-houses (the other, of course, is Sotheby's, see p50) are both based in London. Christie's has been helping collectors build up, and, in later generations dispose of, great collections of pictures and furniture since 1766. Except for the very, very grandest sales (to which admission is restricted to those who have bought catalogues), you are welcome to have a look at the goods to be auctioned in the four days before the sale and, indeed, to attend the auction itself – one of the best free shows in town.
/ Times: Mon-Fri 9.30-16.30 (Tue 20.00); Sun 14.00-16.30; Tube: Green Park.

Concord Lighting WC1
174 High Holborn   0171-497 1400   2–2C

If you are walking around the centre of town, perhaps on your way to Covent Garden (see also), pause to look in the huge windows of this building. If the extravagant installations intrigue you sufficiently that you want to get closer, you can. Visitors are welcome in what is actually the foyer of a lighting company. / Times: Mon-Fri 09.30-17.00; Tube: Holborn.

Contemporary Applied Art W1
2 Percy St   0171-436 2344   2–1C

At Britain's largest gallery specialising in the exhibition and sale of contemporary crafts you find jewellery, fine metalwork, ceramics, wood, textiles, furniture, glass and paper. Eight exhibitions are held a year – they are free but as everything is for sale your visit could turn out to be expensive!
/ Times: Mon-Sat 10.30-17.30; Tube: Goodge Street, Tottenham Court Road.

Flaxman Gallery WC1
University College, Gower St   0171-380 7793   2–1C

John Flaxman (1755–1826) was a pre-eminent name in the emergence of neo-classicism in England and was, in 1810, appointed the first Professor of Sculpture at the Royal Academy. The gallery, inaugurated in 1857, displays many of the plaster models from which the marble sculptures were made. / Times: Mon-Thu 8.45-10.30, Fri 8.45-19.00, Sat 09.30-16.30; Tube: Warren Street, Goodge Street.

Fortnum & Mason W1
181 Piccadilly   0171-734 8040   2–2B

The royal grocers (established on this site in 1707) have all the accoutrements you could possibly desire of such an establishment – plush red carpets, glittering chandeliers and assistants in tailcoats. The shop has particularly impressive displays of its produce, both in the grand ground floor sales area and in the Piccadilly windows. The shop's clock is a well-known landmark – see the outdoor section. / Times: Mon-Sat 09.30-18.00; Tube: Green Park, Piccadilly Circus.

Foyle's WC2

113-119 Charing Cross Rd   0171-437 5660   2–2C

You can potter happily for hours in Britain's biggest bookshop – an establishment which carries a copy of almost every book in print, however esoteric. Actually finding any given title may, however, prove a little difficult. / *Times: Mon-Sat 09.00-18.00 (19.00 Thu); Tube: Tottenham Court Road, Leicester Square.*

Freemason's Hall WC2

Great Queen St   0171-831 9811   2–2D

If you have always been fascinated by the aura of secrecy of Freemasonry, it may come as a surprise that the Masons are very pleased for you to visit their daunting Grand Temple in Covent Garden. The current monolith was dedicated in 1933, but the site has been associated with Freemasonry for over two centuries. The Library and Museum (with collections of plate, glassware, jewels, regalia and Masonic memorabilia) are open to the public. Generally, from Monday to Friday, 11.00 to 16.00, but not 13.00, there are hourly tours which include one of the temples (perhaps even the Grand Temple), but call before you set off. Tours are available on Saturday by arrangement. / *Times: Mon-Fri 10.00-17.00, Sat 10.00-13.00; Tube: Holborn, Covent Garden.*

Grant Museum of Zoology and Comparative Anatomy WC1

Biology Department (Darwin Building), University College, Gower St   0171-387 7050 ext 2647   2–1C

The some 35,000 specimens in this natural history collection range across the animal kingdom from an aardvark through gorillas and sloths to a quagga (an extinct type of zebra). There are skeletons, specimens in jars and stuffed things. Although primarily a teaching hospital, it is open to anyone by appointment and is popular with photographers and artists. School groups are also welcome. / *Times: by appointment: write to, or call, Helen Chatterjee (e-mail hchatterjee@ucl.ac.uk); Tube: Euston Square, Euston, Warren or Goodge Street (or rail, Euston).*

Great Ormond Street Hospital for Children WC1

Peter Pan Gallery, 55 Great Ormond St
0171-405 9200   2–1D

The potted history of this famous hospital, founded in 1852, is the subject of an exhibition in a Georgian townhouse opposite the main building. Exhibits include photographs and ephemera such as patient admission cards and old surgical tools. Since 1929 the hospital has received the copyright proceeds from sales of J M Barrie's Peter Pan and there are letters from the author as well as copies of the book in a number of languages. / *Times: by appointment, 09.30-16.30; Tube: Russell Square, Holborn, Euston.*

Hamleys W1
188 Regent St   0171-734 3161   2–2B
At Christmas it's unbearably crowded, but, year round, this is the number one destination on any child's tour of London – the world's largest toyshop. / Times: Mon-Sat 10.00-19.00 (sometimes longer hours), Sun 12.00-18.00; Tube: Piccadilly Circus, Oxford Circus.

Harrods SW1
Knightsbridge   0171-730 1234   3–1D
Europe's most famous department store works very hard to ensure there is always something new to see in its 25 acres of sales space. First-time visitors should not miss the Food Halls, with their intriguing décor and amazing arrangements of produce, but it is the sheer scale of the whole building and the opulence of some of the goods which are probably the main attractions. Special exhibitions are sometimes organised in the ground floor Central Hall. Harrods is a little sensitive about its role as a free tourist attraction – parties of four or more are not admitted, dress should be appropriate and photography is not allowed. / Times: Mon, Tue & Sat 10.00-18.00, Wed-Fri 10.00-19.00; Tube: Knightsbridge.

Harvey Nichols SW1
Knightsbridge   0171-235 5000   3–1D
Harvey Nichols is a smaller, more intimate department store than its better-known Knightsbridge neighbour and not, therefore, quite as suited to sightseeing. The particularly innovative window displays are always interesting, though, and the glamorous new foodie complex on the fifth floor is worth a look for the sheer improbability of its Dan Dare-style architecture and location. / Times: Mon-Fri 10.00-19.00 (Wed 20.00), Sat 10.00-18.00, Sun 12.00-17.00; Tube: Knightsbridge.

Heinz Gallery, RIBA W1
21 Portman Square   0171-307 3628   2–2A
The exhibitions shown here are described as "looking backward" at the historical aspects of architecture in contrast to the Architecture Centre (see also) which looks forward. The "darkly elegant room" (to use the organisation's own phrase) is the setting for about six shows a year which are diverse in their inspiration, and unlikely to be so large as to overwhelm those without a specialist interest. / Times: Mon-Fri 11.00-17.00, Sat 10.00-13.00; Tube: Marble Arch, Baker Street.

Houses of Parliament SW1
0171-219 4272   2–3C

No visitor will wish to miss the sight of the Palace of Westminster, with its famous clock tower (whose bell is known as Big Ben). There has been a royal palace here since the c11, but, after a disastrous fire in 1835, the building was reconstructed in neo-Gothic style to the designs of Charles Barry and Augustus Pugin. Only Westminster Hall (facing Parliament Green) retains a significant medieval element.

The building is not generally open to the public, but if you want to see the fine interior – or our ancient democracy at work – there are two ways of going about it. One is to arrange to go on a tour and the other is to watch a debate – in the Commons or Lords (from one of the Strangers' Galleries) or in a Commons committee. Dealing with the former first, UK citizens wanting a tour must apply to their MP in writing, and should do so well in advance. Citizens of other countries may apply, in writing, to the Public Information Office of the House of Commons (and may be accommodated at shorter notice).

If you want to watch a debate in progress, the galleries are open to the public. However, priority is given to those with tickets, and the safest course, therefore, to avoid a lengthy queue, is to apply for a ticket, as far in advance as possible, to your MP (or, if you are not a UK citizen, to your embassy or High Commission). Impromptu visitors have a good chance of gaining admission (unless the subject of debate is very controversial) later on in the day – sittings usually go on until 22.00, and sometimes beyond – or on Friday.

If you're planning a visit to Parliament, you can check out your plans with the Public Information Office on the number given. / Tube: Westminster.

Liberty W1
214-220 Regents St   0171-734 1234   2–2B

Liberty is one of the most charming and individualistic of London's department stores. It occupies very characterful mock-Tudor premises (built in the '20s, from timbers from men o'war), which are certainly worth a look. The store's particular strength is house furnishings and it carries many interesting and unusual objects and fabrics. / Times: Mon-Sat 10.00-18.30 (Thu 19.30), Sun 12.00-18.00; Tube: Piccadilly Circus.

London Scottish Regimental Museum SW1
95 Horseferry Rd   0171-630 1639   2–4C
The collection covers what the Regiment wore and fought with since its formation in 1859. Exhibits include medals (the regiment has three VCs to its credit), the three war memorials in the Drill Hall, badges, an indexed record of previous members as well as hundreds of photos documenting the history of the Regiment. / Times: by (telephone) appointment; Tube: St James's.

Museum of Mankind W1
6 Burlington Gardens   0171-437 2224   2–2B
The Mayfair outpost of the British Museum, is a huge Victorian edifice (originally the HQ of London University) housing its collections relating to non-Western societies and cultures. The changing exhibitions are illustrated by occasional gallery talks and lectures. Videos are shown at 13.30 and 15.00 (Tue-Fri). / Times: Mon-Sat 10.00-17.00, Sun 14.30-18.00; Tube: Piccadilly Circus; Café.

National Gallery WC2
Trafalgar Square   0171-389 1785
(recorded information 0171-839 3526)   2–2C
One of the world's great galleries of Western European paintings, from the late c13 to the early c20 – from Giotto to Picasso. What distinguishes it is the balance of its collection across all of the schools, with practically no great master unrepresented.

The Sainsbury Wing (1991) houses the earliest works (including Botticelli, Bellini, Raphael), and the rest of the collection progresses chronologically through the West Wing (Michelangelo, Holbein, Titian), the North Wing (Rubens, Velázquez, Rembrandt) and the East Wing (Gainsborough, Turner, Constable, Monet, van Gogh). The Beggruen collection beefs up the gallery's own Post-Impressionist collection, and includes works by Cézanne, Seurat and Braque.

Tours of the collection take place two or three times daily (Mon-Sat), according to the season, and there are lectures at 13.00 (Tue-Fri) and 12.00 (Sat). At 13.00 on Monday, there are films about artists or schools of painting, while on Tuesday and Thursday lunchtimes and weekend afternoons there are free lectures: for information, pick up a copy of The National Gallery News. *If you prefer to let your fingers do the walking (or have a child, of any age, to amuse), don't miss the Micro Gallery Computer Information Room. Kids will also like the excellent free guide/trail,* Children's Way In. *There is a charge for some of the special exhibitions. (Note that the cloakrooms here won't keep packages or bags.)* / Times: Mon-Sun 10.00-18.00; Tube: Charing Cross, Leicester Square; Café.

Central London

National Portrait Gallery WC2
2 St Martin's Place   0171-306 0055   2–2C
This is arguably the most accessible of London's major galleries. Though in most collections it's artistic merit which wins a place, here it's the importance of the subject of the portrait as much as the eminence of the painter, sculptor or photographer (though many of the great British artists are, of course, represented). Almost all the major figures of English history are recorded, organised by period, with the contemporary portraiture galleries being the most popular. The galleries and holdings of the Victorian and early c20 portraits were redesigned in late 1996 to "visually and intellectually stimulate the visitor". On Tuesdays to Fridays at 13.10 (Sat & Sun, 15.00), there is a lecture on some aspect of the collection. There are a variety of temporary exhibitions, for some of which there is a charge. / Times: Mon-Sat 10.00-18.00, Sun 12.00-18.00; Tube: Leicester Square, Charing Cross.

Percival David Foundation of Chinese Art WC1
53 Gordon Square   0171-387 3909   2–1C
The finest collection of Chinese ceramics outside China is not nearly as well known as it deserves. There are approximately 1,700 items of ceramics, reflecting Chinese court taste from the c10 to c18. Two of the particular treasures are a unique pair of blue and white temple vases whose inscriptions date them to 1351. / Times: Mon-Fri 10.30-17.00; Tube: Russell Square, Goodge Street, Euston Square.

Petrie Museum of Egyptian Archaeology WC1
University College, Gower St   0171-387 7050   2–1C
An extraordinary collection of Egyptian antiquities, excavated by the eminent archaeologist Sir Flinders Petrie and his followers since 1884. The exhibition is organised to illustrate the development of Egyptian culture from Palaeolithic to Roman and Coptic times. / Times: Mon-Fri 10.00-12.00, 13.15-17.00; closed four weeks in summer; open three Sats each year, officially for Friends of the Museum; Tube: Warren Street, Goodge Street.

Phillips W1
101 New Bond St   0171-629 6602   2–2B
It may be a little less well known than Sotheby's and Christie's, but this Mayfair auctioneer offers just the same possibilities of getting close to great (and lesser) works of art. (For an introduction to the auction houses, see Christie's.) Items range from furniture to textiles and viewings and sales are free, as are verbal valuations if you have an item you feel (or hope) may be of value. / Times: Mon-Fri 08.30-17.00; Sun 14.00-17.00; Bayswater also Sat 09.00-12.30; Tube: Bond Street.

The Photographers' Gallery WC2

5 & 8 Great Newport St   0171-831 1772   2–2C
This large, central gallery maintains an ever-changing programme of photographic exhibitions. Details of occasional free tours and forthcoming events are listed in the free magazine, Great. / Times: Mon-Sat 11.00-18.00;
Tube: Leicester Square; Café.

Royal Academy of Arts * W1

Burlington House, Piccadilly   0171-439 7438   2–2B
Although there is a charge for all of the exhibitions (of which the most famous is the annual Summer Exhibition), there is no fee to access the Academy's charming building, and two of its greatest attractions – one architectural, one artistic – which are always on view gratis.

The Sackler Galleries (built 1990) are reckoned by many to be one of the most successful modern additions to any period London building. The glass-sided lift, by which the new galleries are approached, offers a magical journey from the old to the new, and some of the Academy's sculptures are dramatically displayed outside the galleries. At the far end, in its own white space, is displayed the Academy's greatest artistic treasure, the Michelangelo Tondo – the only example in England of the master's sculpture. There are periodic free tours of the early c18 Private Rooms, which are the most characterful part of the Academy – you need to book in advance. / Times: 10.00-18.00; Tube: Piccadilly Circus, Green Park; Café.

Royal College of Physicians NW1

11 St Andrew's Place, Regent's Park
0171-935 1174   4–4B
This art-based collection includes exhibits dating back to the c16. These include: portraits, such as William Harvey, who discovered the circulation of the blood; slides and photographs; busts; medals and miniatures. There are also thousands of original engravings, all catalogued, of medical personalities. The works are of interest to people researching family history where relatives have been fellows of the College, and the building attracts students of architecture. The College is in a row of Regency Nash buildings, but dates from 1964, and was designed by Sir Denys Lasdun. The Census Room contains the c17 wooden panelling taken from the original home of the College. / Times: entry by appointment with the librarian; Tube: Regent's Park, Great Portland St.

Royal Courts of Justice WC2
Strand   0171-936 6000   2–2D

Almost all the most important civil cases in England and Wales end up being tried in this imposing Victorian Gothic building. There are usually at least 50 courts sitting at any one time so you should be able to find something of interest. Trials might cover anything from allocating fault for a serious accident to esoteric 'administrative' law cases, in which people can challenge the government's exercise of its powers. Children under 16 are not admitted. / Times: Mon-Fri 10.00-16.00; Tube: Temple; Café.

Royal Institution W1
21 Albemarle St   0171-409 2992   2–2B

As they are often televised, you may well have seen the annual Christmas lectures given at this huge Mayfair institution (where Faraday 'discovered' electricity). While there is a charge for these lectures, the society provides two free lunchtime talks per year, one in November and one in March, both 13.00-13.40. There are also several much less formal evening discussions per term (Sep, Dec and Jan-Apr), and sometimes one or more in the summer. The evening events take the form of a lecture by an expert followed by questions from the audience. Recent lunchtime subjects have included Ozone Depletion while evening topics have covered 'Artificial Intelligence' and asked, 'Is there life on Mars?' The building has been home to the Institution (founded in 1799) for nearly 200 years; it contains the world's oldest working science laboratory and a museum. Entry is free for both and tours can be arranged. / Tube: Green Park.

Royal Mint Sovereign Galleries SW1
7 Grosvenor Gardens   0171-931 7977   2–4B

A new gallery in a large Victorian townhouse illustrating the 500-year history of gold sovereigns. It is housed in two interconnecting rooms, one of which contains many valuable and glittering items. / Times: Mon-Fri 10.00-16.00 (groups may also be accommodated outside these hours); Tube: Victoria.

Royal Society of Art WC2
8 John Adam St   0171-930 5115   2–2C

The Royal Society for the encouragement of Arts, Manufactures and Commerce, (to give it its full name) organises around 40 lectures a year. They are aimed at members but the public are welcome to attend if they apply in advance for a ticket. The range of subjects is wide including, 'The Adam and Eve Theories' and 'A Peck of Dirt: are we too hygienic?', through to talks on topical political, social or business issues. There are also a couple of lectures each year for children, often on a technological theme. / Tube: Embankment.

St Martin-in-the-Fields WC2
Trafalgar Square   0171-930 1862   2–2C
*One of the grandest of London's churches – well, its parish
does include Buckingham Palace – and a particularly fine
sight when floodlit. It was designed by James Gibbs and
completed in 1726. There are one-hour concerts every
weekday (except Wed & Thu) at 13.05 – a perfect break
from one of the most hectic parts of London or a suitable
finale to a visit to the neighbouring National Gallery (see
also). On Wednesday & Sunday, there is a choral evensong at
17.00.* / Times: 08.00-18.00; Tube: Charing Cross, Piccadilly Circus; Café.

Salvation Army International
Heritage Centre WC1
117-121 Judd St   0171-387 1656   4–3C
*Discover what inspired William Booth to devote his life to the
poor and homeless – the history of the Salvation Army from
1865 is the subject of this exhibition at the Army's King's
Cross headquarters. A one-hour recorded tour of the
exhibition is available at no charge.* / Times: Mon-Fri 09.30-15.30,
Sat 09.30-12.30; Tube: King's Cross.

Shane English School W1
59 South Molton St   0171-499 8533   2–2B
*If you're not a native speaker, you can learn or improve your
English for free on a course in Central London. Every four
weeks a new intake of teachers on a month-long programme
leading to a recognised qualification of teaching English as a
foreign language need a class to practise on. Around 15
places are available at elementary and intermediate levels.
Would-be students must commit themselves for the full
duration and pay a £20 deposit which they receive back on
completion of the course.* / Times: Mon-Fri 14.00-16.30; Tube: Bond
Street.

Sir John Soane's Museum * WC2
13 Lincoln's Inn Fields   0171-430 0175 (infoline)
0171-405 2107   2–1D
*One of the most extraordinary buildings in the world, this is
actually three linked townhouses. It was built by the great
architect between 1812 and 1837 for his own occupation
and as a home for his eclectic collection of treasures. These
include important (and sometimes fascinating) artefacts from
Egyptian, Greek and Roman civilisations. There are also
pictures, most famously Hogarth's series of paintings,
The Rake's Progress. The greatest attraction, however, is just
wandering around this labyrinthine house, which you may do
without any charge (though you do have to pay for conducted
tours and special exhibitions).* / Times: Tue-Sat 10.00-17.00, 1st Tue of
month 18.00-21.00; Tube: Holborn.

Sotheby's W1

34-35 New Bond St   0171-493 8080   2–2B

Sotheby's is possibly the best known of the great international art auctioneers. Details of access are broadly as for its competitor, Christie's (see also). / Times: Mon-Fri 09.00-16.30, occasional weekend viewing; Tube: Bond Street, Green Park; Café.

Tate Gallery SW1

Millbank   0171-887 8000   2–4C

The Tate occupies a particularly charming building overlooking the Thames. It is really two galleries, combining, as it does, the functions of national galleries of British Art (from the c16) and of international c20 art. Most British artists of any repute are represented, and the Blake and Hogarth collections are particularly fine. The Clore Galleries house the enormous Turner Bequest.

Great masters of modern art well represented include Francis Bacon and there are some key works by Picasso. The gallery is re-hung every year. There are tours of different parts of the collection weekdays at 11.00, 12.00, 14.00 and 15.00; and at 15.00 on Saturday there is a tour of the highlights of the collection. There are lectures at 13.00 (Tue-Sat) and 14.30 (Sun), and there are films (Wed-Sat, at 14.30 and Sun at 15.45), not always of the esoteric sort in which most museums specialise. Almost all the Tate's attractions are free of charge, with the exception of the three big annual shows. In 2000, a new Tate Gallery opens at Bankside; meanwhile the Tate Gallery of Modern Art Visitor Centre (see also) informs visitors what they have to look forward to and keeps them up to date with progress on the building. / Times: Mon-Sun 10.00-18.00; Tube: Pimlico; Café.

Twinings WC2

216 Strand   0171-353 3511   2–2D

Dating from 1706, the shop of the famous tea company claims to be the oldest in London in its original ownership, and selling the same product. It certainly has a lot of period charm and its compact premises (suitable for small parties only) house a collection illustrating the history of Twinings and its involvement in tea. / Times: Mon-Fri 09.30-16.30 (and the morning of the Sat of the Lord Mayor's Show); Tube: Temple.

University College Art Collection WC1

Strang Print Room, University College, Gower St
0171-387 7050   2–1C

Works on paper are the particular strength of this collection of 8,000 items, which also includes paintings and sculpture. There is no permanent exhibition, and to show off the works a programme of temporary shows is organised. A catalogue is available and a web-site is planned. / Times: Mon-Fri 13.00-17.00 during term time; Tube: Warren Street, Goodge Street.

Wallace Collection W1
Manchester Square   0171-935 0687   2–1A
Hertford House, an imposing and sumptuous mansion just north of Oxford Street, contains one of the most splendid collections of paintings and artefacts in London. It has been suggested that Gallery 24, with its works by Watteau and Fragonard, houses the finest group of French c18 pictures which can be seen in a single room anywhere. The collection also includes works by Rembrandt, Rubens and Hals (Laughing Cavalier). Extraordinary clocks, Sèvres porcelain and armour are among the other attractions. / Times: Mon-Sat 10.00-17.00, Sun 11.00-17.00 (Sep-Mar, Sun 14.00-17.00); Tube: Bond Street.

Westminster Abbey * SW1
0171-222 5152   2–3C
There is no building in England as historic as this great church, whose consecration predated the Invasion of 1066 by a few months, and which has been the setting for every Coronation since. Unfortunately, the strain of accommodating around 2.5 million visitors a year means it can be difficult to find peace to appreciate the magnificent architecture (mainly c13 to c16) or to explore the numerous tombs and memorials. (Among the famous people buried here are Elizabeth I, Mary Queen of Scots, Chaucer, Dickens and Newton.) The cloisters and nave (the latter is free to individuals, though there is a charge for groups) are always open – subject to services – but there is a charge to visit the Royal Chapels. A good way to get some tranquillity while admiring the building is to attend the short weekly organ recital at 17.45 on Sunday or one of the many services (Mon-Fri at 17.00, Sat/Sun 15.00), and at evensong, (except Wed, when it is said) you can hear the Abbey's very fine choir. / Times: Mon-Fri 09.00-16.45, Sat 09.00-14.45 & 15.45-17.45; Tube: Westminster, St James's.

Westminster Cathedral SW1
Victoria St   0171-798 9055   2–4C
Completed in 1903, this Byzantine-style Roman Catholic cathedral houses some fine marble work and mosaics, with the sculptures of the 14 Stations of the Cross by Eric Gill being particularly renowned. The cathedral is famous for its choir, and services are sung daily except in August. Unfortunately there is a small charge to ascend the campanile (bell tower), which gives a fine view over much of London. Visitors cannot explore while services are in progress. / Times: Mon-Fri 07.00-19.00, Sat 08.00-19.00; Tube: Victoria.

Outdoor attractions

Buckingham Palace * SW1
0171-930 4832   2–3B
This house has been the principal residence of the Sovereign only since Victoria's day. You know if Her Majesty is at home because the royal standard flies when she is in residence. The main façade, facing the Mall, is much more recent (1913) than the rest of the building and, as is often noted, gives the impression of nothing so much as a more-important-than-usual branch of Barclays Bank. To get a better feeling of what lies behind the façade walk down Buckingham Gate and appreciate the side view of the palace. The Queen's private quarters are on the other side, overlooking Constitution Hill. (There is a charge for the summer tours of the interior of the palace, as there is for admission to the Queen's Gallery or the Royal Mews.) One of the best times to visit, of course, is for the Changing of the Guard (see also). / Tube: St James's Park, Victoria, Green Park.

Cleopatra's Needle WC2
Victoria Embankment   2–2D
This 3,500-year-old obelisk was taken from near the Temple of the Sun God in Heliopolis in Egypt and was presented to Britain by the Turkish Viceroy in 1819. It has a twin, which stands in New York's Central Park. / Tube: Embankment.

Coram's Fields WC1
93 Guilford St   0171-837 6138   2–1D
Seven acres of central London to which adults (over 16) are not admitted – unless accompanied by a child! This shady playground – a legacy of an c18 philanthropist – is a boon for harassed parents. It boasts play equipment, a sports area, paddling pool, pets corner and a duck pond. / Times: 09.00-20.00 (Easter to end Oct) or dusk (winter); Tube: Russell Square; Café school holidays only.

Covent Garden WC2
0171-836 9136   2–2C
Covent Garden, with its c18 market-setting and its colourful shops, stalls and cafés, is one of the most agreeable and popular places for a stroll in central London. There's almost invariably something going on in the way of busking or more serious street theatre – the Market office (on the number given) can provide information about forthcoming attractions. / Tube: Covent Garden, Leicester Square; Café.

Eros SW1
Piccadilly Circus   2–2C
Although invariably known as Eros, the famous, small statue at Piccadilly Circus (the world's first to be made of aluminium) in fact represents the Angel of Christian Charity, and commemorates Lord Shaftesbury, whose Avenue is nearby. / Tube: Piccadilly Circus.

Fortnum & Mason Clock W1
181 Piccadilly   2–2B
On the hour, every hour, four-foot figures of Mr Fortnum and Mr Mason emerge from doors above the shop's main entrance, face each other and bow. A c18 air is then played on 17 bells. The two gentlemen then bow again and retire to their respective quarters. All in all, it's quite an amusing performance from one of London's few performing clocks. (See also Swiss Centre.) / Tube: Piccadilly Circus.

Green Park SW1
0171-930 1793   2–3B
The park was originally meadowland used for the chase, and duels were regularly fought here until the mid c17. Now the 53 acres by Piccadilly comprise what the unkind might describe as the Cinderella of the Royal Parks – alone among them, it lacks a lake, flowers, summer music and café. It is, however, a relaxing place and very central. / Times: 24 hours; Tube: Green Park, Hyde Park Corner; Café.

Old Bond Street W1
2–2B
If you're seriously into window-shopping, you certainly shouldn't miss the extraordinary row of shops to be found in this street. For more than three centuries, this has been London's most fashionable boutique thoroughfare – all the shops whose very names conjure up wild extravagance are there. / Tube: Green Park.

Riverside Walk
See the South section for suggestions of interesting walks by the Thames.

Roman Bath * WC2
5 Strand Ln   0171-798 2064   2–2D
A whodunnit (or rather 'who built it') mystery surrounds the remains of a bath restored in c17 and believed by some people to be Roman. It's owned by the National Trust (and there is an entry fee), but if you find your way down the steps and into the narrow lane, 90 per cent of what there is to see is visible through the window. / Times: 24 hours (light switch operational from outside); Tube: Temple (not Sun), Blackfriars, Charing Cross.

St James's Park SW1
0171-930 1793   2–3C
This is possibly the most beautiful, and certainly the most highly cultivated, of the Royal Parks. Situated in the ceremonial heart of London, between Westminster and Buckingham Palace, it offers idyllic views. During the summer, there are frequent concerts at the bandstand, and the pelicans are fed at 15.00 every afternoon, by Duck Island. / Times: 24 hours; Tube: St James's Park; Café.

Speakers' Corner W2
Hyde Park (NE corner)   2–2A
For more than a century, this has been the London home of the soapbox orator – Sunday sees the expression of a kaleidoscope of views, from the slightly off-beat to the decidedly cranky. / Times: Sun afternoon; Tube: Marble Arch.

Swiss Centre Clock W1
Leicester Square   2–2C
The Swiss Centre boasts a fine 27-bell glockenspiel, which plays Brahms, classical Swiss folk tunes and other folk music from around the world. It was built and dedicated to the City of Westminster to celebrate the latter's 400th anniversary in 1985. Performances at noon, 18.00, 19.00 and 20.00 every day, and, at weekends and bank holidays on the hour every hour, between noon and 20.00, except 13.00.
/ Tube: Piccadilly Circus.

Trafalgar Square WC2
Trafalgar Square   2–2C
This great, central square is most famous for its 170-foot column dedicated to the memory of Lord Nelson (1843), its fountains and its pigeons. The statues of imperial lions (Landseer, 1867) are also well known, despite the fact that real lions never sit as represented – they always lie on their side. / Tube: Leicester Square, Charing Cross.

Victoria Embankment Gardens WC2
Villiers St   2–2D
Festivals details: Alternative Arts 0171-375 0441   2–2D
This elongated park with its profusion of blooms in spring offers many events, for example, dance, mime, music, poetry and opera festivals, street theatre and a Disability Arts Cabaret. In spite its attraction as a central site of free entertainment, it is quite peaceful, considering the major road running alongside (though it is very popular with local office workers at lunchtimes). It is the site of York Watergate (1626) and there are many plaques and explanatory notices to educate you. / Tube: Charing Cross; Café.

Victoria Tower Gardens SW1
Millbank   2–4C
This quiet and extremely scenic garden, beneath the looming presence of the Victoria Tower (at the other end of the Houses of Parliament from Big Ben) is graced by a cast of Rodin's Burghers of Calais and by a bronze of the Suffragette, Emmeline Pankhurst. / Times: 07.00-dusk; Tube: Westminster.

West London

Introduction

West London offers a lot of possibilities to those who want to combine a little artistic or intellectual interest (perhaps a trip to the **Victoria and Albert Museum**, the **Serpentine Gallery** or the **National Sound Archive**) with a visit to one of the beautiful parks which dot the area, such as **Hyde Park, Kensington Gardens** and **Holland Park.**

This combination makes it an excellent area for days out with children, for whom the **Natural History** and **Science Museums** are top attractions. Both those museums are open free of charge only later in the day so it makes sense to do a park first, and to finish on an educational note.

Away from the centre and its famous parks, the area is rich with fine houses and gardens such as **Osterley Park, Chiswick House** and **Hampton Court**. Take a picnic, and all should – if the weather is fine – provide a good day out. All are close to the **Riverside Walk**, either for a stroll after lunch or for some more serious exercise.

For those who prefer to amble in a more urban, or accessible, environment the pleasures of Saturday's Portobello Road market are hard to beat.

Some lesser-known central attractions well worth investigating include the **Royal Hospital** (and the neighbouring **Ranelagh Gardens**) in Chelsea and **Leighton House Museum and Art Gallery** in **Holland Park**. Further out, **Pitshanger Manor Museum** and **Gunnersbury Park Museum** both offer interesting and attractive houses to visit, set in pleasant parks.

Chelsea Information Office SW3
Old Town Hall, King's Rd   0171-352 6056   3–3C
Chelsea's information office is in the same building as a good reference library; the hours are the same for both. / Times: Mon, Tue & Thu 10.00-20.00 (Wed 13.00, Fri & Sat 17.00); Tube: Sloane Square.

Hillingdon Tourist Information Centre, Middx
Uxbridge Central Library, High St, Uxbridge
01895-250706   off map
The TIC and library keep the same hours. / Times: Mon, Tue & Thu 09.30-20.00, Wed 09.30-17.30, Fri 10.00-17.30, Sat 09.30-16.00; Tube: Uxbridge.

Hounslow Tourist Information Centre, Middx
Treaty Centre, High St, Hounslow
0181-572 8279   off map
 / *Times: Mon-Sat 09.30-17.30, Tue & Thu 09.30-20.00;*
Tube: Hounslow Central.

Twickenham Tourist Information Centre, Middx
Civic Centre, York St, Twickenham
0181-891 7272   off map
 / *Times: Mon-Fri 09.00-17.15 (17.00 Fri); Rail: Twickenham.*

Indoor attractions

Albert Memorial Visitor Centre SW7
Prince's Gate, Kensington Gore   0171-225 1059   3–1B
Since late '94, the Albert Memorial has been shrouded in
scaffolding as conservation takes place before it re-opens in
1999. Now, however, the public can see what has been and is
being done, and what remains to do, at the next door Visitor
Centre. Highlights include a chance to see close up one of the
statues, which is usually 200 feet above ground, and the orb
(complete with 'jewels'). / *Times: Mon-Sun 10.00-18.00;*
Tube: Knightsbridge, South Kensington.

Baden-Powell House SW7
Queen's Gate   0171-584 7030   3–2B
After Baden-Powell's death in 1941, scouts around the world
raised money for a 'living memorial'. The result was this
hostel, opened in 1961. Give at least a week's notice and you
can see the archives, containing records and memorabilia
about the Scout Movement going back to 1907. There is also
what is possibly the world's oldest loaf of bread, along with
material relating to the siege of Mafeking (1899–1900),
and wall displays about aspects of the Movement. / *Times:*
by appointment; Tube: South Kensington, Gloucester Road; Café.

Boston Manor House, Middx
Boston Manor Rd, Brentford   0181-862 7874   off map
This Jacobean manor was built in 1623 and extended in
1670, when it was bought by the Clitherow family, whose
home it remained until 1924. The first floor State Rooms
have English Renaissance plaster ceilings. The early c19
ground floor rooms house paintings which relate to the
locality. / *Times: from 1st Sat in Apr to last Sun in Oct – Sat, Sun & Bank Hol*
Mon 14.30-17.00; Tube: Boston Manor.

British Optical Association Museum SW5

c/o The College of Optometrists, 10 Knaresbrough Place
0171-373 7765   3–2A

*One JH Sutcliffe, a passionate collector of spectacles and
other optical devices, was the original creator of this museum,
some of whose artefacts are three centuries old. Highlights
include leather-framed c17 designs, opthalmoscopes and
highly decorated opera glasses and lorgnettes.*
/ Times: 10.00-16.00 (by appointment); Tube: Earls Court, Gloucester Road.

Cat Museum, Middx

49 High St, Harrow-on-the-Hill   0181-422 1892   off map
*Antique models of cats from around the world – represented
in every medium from pottery, through paintings, to prints
and wood – are the subject of this idiosyncratic collection.*
/ Times: Thu-Sat 09.30-17.00; Tube: Harrow-on-the-Hill.

Czech Memorial Scrolls Centre SW7

Westminster Synagogue, Kent House, Rutland Gardens
0171-584 3741   3–1C

*In 1964, 1564 Torah scrolls were rescued from communist
Prague. This exhibition tells their story and something of the
history of the communities they came from. It describes the
retrieval of the scrolls and their subsequent restoration and
dispersal. Beautifully decorated Torah mantels are also on
display.* / Times: Tue & Thu 10.00-16.00 (closed some days in Jun & Jul);
Tube: Knightsbridge.

Gillette UK, Middx

Great West Rd, Isleworth   0181-560 1234
(ask for Richard Wildgoose)   off map

*The reception area of this famous manufacturer of razors
(and now toiletries) houses showcases for an ever-expanding
collection of the company's products. The most interesting
aspect of the collection is the stories that accompany some of
the items, which include razors belonging to soldiers who
served in WWI, and Sir Thomas Lipton, the tea magnate.*
/ Times: individuals, by appointment, during working hours, groups (must be
small), by appointment outside of these times; Rail: Syon Park.

Goethe Institute SW7

50 Princes Gate, Exhibition Rd   0171-411 3400
Library 0171-411 3452   3–1C

*The Institute has a small gallery which has changing
exhibitions of works by artists from Germany or those
connected in some other way with the country. Small parties
(one or two people) can pre-book to view a video from the
extensive collection – the wide range includes documentaries
and dramas.* / Times: Mon-Thu 10.00-20.00, Fri 10.00-16.00, Sat
09.30-12.30; library 11.00-20.00, closed Fri & Sat 10.00-13.00;
Tube: South Kensington; Café.

Gunnersbury Park Museum W3

Gunnersbury Park, Popes Lane   0181-992 1612   1–3A
This very grand local museum recently celebrated 70 years of opening to the public. It houses a large local collection but also temporary exhibitions on wider themes. Housed in a former Rothschild family house, built in 1835 on the site of a former royal residence, it benefits from an extremely pleasant park location and on summer weekends you can see the original Victorian kitchens. / Times: Apr-Oct 13.00-17.00 (Sat, Sun & Bank Hol -18.00); Nov-Mar 13.00-16.00; kitchens (summer only) 13.00-16.00; Tube: Acton Town; Café summer only.

Heathrow Airport, Middx

Hounslow   Visitors centre 0181-745 6655
brochure line 01233-211207   off map
Heathrow is staggering in the scale of its operations, handling nearly 55 million passengers a year (and more international passengers than any other airport in the world). There is a Visitors Centre, a viewing gallery and an exhibition with interactive technology; worksheets are available for children and, for all ages, there are free self-guided tours, with headsets. From the viewing area in Terminal 2, you can watch all the comings and goings. Call the brochure line for a helpful leaflet that explains the functions of the buildings and contains a plane spotter's guide to tail markings. / Times: 09.00-30 mins before dusk; Tube: Heathrow Terminals 1,2,3,4.

Hillingdon Local Heritage Service, Middx

Uxbridge Central Library, High St, Uxbridge
01895-250702   off map
The borough doesn't have a dedicated museum but makes do with a small display space in the Central Library. Here you find changing exhibitions and a local studies room. There are periodic events and also workshops for children. / Times: main library: Mon, Tue & Thu 09.30-20.00, Wed 09.30-17.30, Fri 10.00-17.30, Sat 09.30-16.00; local studies library Mon 09.30-20.00, Tue-Thu 13.00-17.30, Fri 10.00-17.30, Sat 09.30-12.00 & 13.00-16.00; Tube: Uxbridge.

Hogarth's House W4

Hogarth Lane, Great West Rd   0181-994 6757   1–3A
The Chiswick home of the great English engraver and painter William Hogarth (1697-1764) has been newly restored to celebrate the tercentenary of his birth. It contains memorabilia of his life, work and circle. The main attractions, however, are his most famous series of engravings (such as Marriage à la Mode and the Rake's Progress) and the attractive garden, which contains a mulberry tree dating from the painter's time. / Times: Tue-Fri 13.00-17.00 (Nov-Mar 16.00); Sat & Sun 13.00-18.00 (Nov-Mar 17.00); Tube: Turnham Green.

Leighton House Museum and Art Gallery W14
12 Holland Park Rd   0171-602 3316   1–3B
No visitor to Holland Park should miss this extraordinary mid-Victorian house, with later Moorish Hall (complete with small pool). It is a wonderful setting for the permanent collection of paintings by Lord Leighton (1830-1896) and some of his contemporaries. In summer the garden, which contains some sculptures, is open. There are also temporary exhibitions in the recently refurbished Perrin Gallery – if you want to assess current standards in what was once London's most famous artistic quarter, don't miss the Kensington and Chelsea Artist's Show in July. / Times: Mon-Sat 11.00-17.30; Tube: High Street Kensington.

Lindsey House SW10
99/100 Cheyne Walk   01494-528051   3–3C
Overlooking the Thames, this building dates from 1674 and is on the site of Sir Thomas More's garden. Despite being owned by the National Trust, it is tenanted, so sightseeing is by appointment only (via the Trust's regional office on the number given) and restricted to the ground floor entrance hall, garden room, main staircase, first floors and gardens. / Times: by appointment; Tube: Sloane Square or South Kensington (both around 1.5 miles).

National Army Museum SW3
Royal Hospital Rd   0171-730 0717   3–3D
The Army's own museum relates its history – from the archers of Henry V to involvement in contemporary UN peacekeeping operations. The emphasis is on the story of the individual soldier, the human aspect. There is a major collection of uniforms, life-sized models in costumes through the ages, paintings of famous battle scenes, portraits by Reynolds and Gainsborough and displays of weaponry and medals. A visit here makes a good fit with a trip to the neighbouring Royal Hospital (see also). / Times: 10.00-17.30; Tube: Sloane Square.

National Sound Archive SW7
29 Exhibition Rd   Library 0171-412 7430;
Sound Archive 0171-412 7441   3–1C
This is one of the largest sound archives in the world. The reception area has a touch screen introduction to the facilities and you can listen to examples of the material held. You can also pick up free leaflets and a newsletter relating to the Archives. There is a library and information service, which includes catalogues of the holdings (both here and, for example, at the BBC), and historical information on recordings. A listening service is also available, by appointment only. / Times: library & listening service Mon-Fri 10.00-17.00 (note library Thu -21.00); Tube: South Kensington.

Natural History Museum * SW7
Cromwell Rd   0171-938 9123   3–2C
Free time is short at this famous museum – at weekends you get only 50 minutes, so may we suggest a few of the key attractions. You will want to spend a few minutes in the cathedral-like central hall, dominated by the skeleton of diplodocus, one of the largest creatures which ever lived. In the remaining time, you might like to take in the dinosaurs exhibition in the new Ronson Gallery, or you might prefer to find out how you, yourself, work, by visiting the Human Biology Gallery. The museum has many interactive displays – it even offers the possibility of 'experiencing' the Kobe earthquake (as felt inside a supermarket) that created havoc in Japan. / Times: Mon-Fri 16.30-17.50; Sat, Sun & Bank Hols 17.00-17.50; Tube: South Kensington.

The Orangery and the Ice House W8
Holland Park   0171-603 1123   3–1A
The charming c18 glasshouse in the centre of Holland Park and the nearby Ice House are used for high quality arts and crafts exhibitions in various media. / Times: 11.00-19.00 (during exhibitions); Tube: High Street Kensington, Holland Park; Café.

Orleans House Gallery, Middx
Riverside, Twickenham   0181-892 0221   off map
Twickenham benefits from an unusually attractive gallery to display its borough art collection and in which to hold temporary, contemporary art exhibitions. The setting, in a picturesque, riverside, woodland garden (open daylight hours), is a good place for a picnic or as a starting point for a stroll along the Thames. / Times: Tue-Sat 13.00-17.30 (winter 16.30), Sun & Bank Hols 14.00-17.30 (winter 16.30); Tube: Richmond.

Pitshanger Manor Museum W5
Mattock Lane, Ealing   0181-567 1227   1–3A
This Ealing house, set in a park, already had the benefit of some exquisite plaster work designed by George Dance in the mid c18, when it attracted the attentions of the great neo-classical architect, Sir John Soane. Between 1800 and 1810, the latter turned the house into a Regency villa. The building (Grade I listed) houses interesting exhibitions. / Times: Tue-Sat 10.00-17.00; Tube: Ealing Broadway; Café.

Polish Institute and Sikorsi Museum SW7
20 Princes Gate   0171-589 9249   3–1C
Anyone with even a passing interest in Poland, or in military history, should visit this elegant museum near Hyde Park – it is by far the most important collection of Polish material anywhere outside that country. There are important mementoes of the many conflicts in which Poles have been involved – for example the national flag flown over the ruins of the monastery of Monte Cassino in 1944, as well as extensive archives. / Times: Mon-Fri 14.00-16.00; 1st Sat of month 10.00-16.00; archives Tue-Fri 10.00-16.00; Tube: South Kensington, Knightsbridge.

Royal College of Art SW7
Kensington Gore   0171-590 4444   3–1B
This is the only exclusively post-graduate university of art and design in the world; famous graduates include David Hockney, Henry Moore and Barbara Hepworth. Courses range from painting, through fashion, to vehicle design. There's almost always an exhibition (and all relate to art and design, including graphic and industrial design) in progress and most are free – but call the Public Relations office before you set out to avoid disappointment. / Times: during exhibitions, Mon-Fri 10.00-18.00; Tube: Knightsbridge, South Kensington.

Royal College of Music – Department of Portraits and Performance History SW7
Prince Consort Rd   0171-591 4340   3–1B
The collections house displays of paintings and busts – of musicians, of course – mainly from the c19 and early c20. There are also hundreds of original watercolours and thousands of engravings and photographs (which are catalogued but not on display, although people with a passion for a particular musical luminary can request to see relevant works). Individuals are welcome. Note: the collection is mainly housed in a gallery on the sixth floor, to which there is no lift. / Times: Mon-Fri by (telephone) appointment; Tube: South Kensington, Gloucester Road.

Royal Hospital SW3
Royal Hospital Rd   0171-730 5282   3–3D
Wren's elegant 1682 building, founded by Charles II for veteran soldiers, is still the home of the Chelsea Pensioners, who can sometimes be spotted around the area wearing their splendid scarlet uniforms. Indeed give a week's notice and a tour, guided by one of the pensioners can be arranged. The Great Hall, the Chapel and the Museum may be visited. Don't miss the lovely grounds, Ranelagh Gardens (see also). / Times: Mon-Sat 10.00-12.00 & 14.00-16.00; Sun (hall & chapel) 14.00-16.00; Tube: Sloane Square.

Royal Military School of Music, Middx
Kneller Hall, Kneller Rd, Twickenham
0181-898 5533   off map
This collection of instruments used by the military includes wind and stringed items from the past three centuries. Of particular interest perhaps is a trumpet taken into the Charge of the Light Brigade, a bugle played at the Battle of Waterloo and indigenous percussion instruments donated by graduating students including 'talking drums' from Africa. Tours can include a visit to the Chapel, the grounds, the museum, and hearing a band in rehearsal. The School is housed in a Jacobean-style mansion, rebuilt in 1854. / Times: by (written) appointment, generally Wed mornings Jun-Aug; Rail: Whitton (10 mins); Café.

Science Museum * SW7
Exhibition Rd   0171-938 8080/8008   3–1C
*Appropriately for the prime technological museum of the first
industrial nation, the exhibits here include many 'firsts': the
first c18 steam engine and the first c19 steam turbine,
Stephenson's train (the Rocket) and the Vickers Vimy aircraft
which made the first non-stop Atlantic crossing in 1919.
There's always a great deal going on throughout the museum,
and there are enough 'hands-on' exhibits in the 40 galleries to
keep children from as young as three happy. There are
charges for some special exhibitions even when entry to the
museum is free. / Times: 16.30-18.00; Tube: South Kensington; Café.*

Serpentine Gallery W2
Kensington Gardens   0171-723 9072   3–1C
*The attractive and popular gallery space in Hyde Park is
scheduled to reopen in September 1997 and offer its first
exhibition in November. It stages a number of modern and
contemporary exhibitions every year. There are usually talks
by artists and critics on Sunday afternoons at 15.00.
/ Times: during exhibitions, 10.00-18.00; Tube: Lancaster Gate; Café.*

Victoria & Albert Museum * SW7
Cromwell Rd   0171-938 8500   3–2C
*The V&A holds the world's greatest collection of decorative
arts and design. Ceramics, furniture and dress are but three
examples of the fields in which it holds comprehensive
collections, and the museum is also home to the national
collections of photography and watercolours. The refurbished
Raphael Gallery contains seven tapestries sometimes claimed
to be among the greatest national treasures. The galleries
housing the collection of English silver from 1300-1800,
also reopened recently. Free family trails on Indian, Korean
and Gothic displays are available from Information Desks.
/ Times: Mon-Sun 16.30-17.50; Tube: South Kensington.*

Wilkinson Sword Museum W3
19-21 Brunel Rd   0181-749 1061   1–2A
*Take a tour, and you can see swords still being made at this
company more generally today associated with razors. A small
museum-cum-showroom includes historic and new swords,
and guns from the c18. Groups (maximum of eight) are
preferred. (The introduction of a charge was being considered
at the time of writing.) / Times: by appointment; Tube: East Acton.*

William Morris Society W6
Kelmscott House, 26 Upper Mall   0181-741 3735   1–3A
*Occupying part of the house in which Morris – socialist,
designer and author – lived from 1878 until his death in
1896, this small collection of memorabilia, designs and books
includes one of the original presses on which his novels,
poetry and pamphlets were printed. Devotees should also see
the entry for the William Morris Gallery in the East End.
/ Times: Thu & Sat 14.00-17.00; Tube: Ravenscourt Park.*

Outdoor attractions

Burnham Beeches, Bucks
Farnham Common   01753-647358   off map
One of the finest examples of ancient woodland in Britain, owned by the Corporation of London for more than a century. The most famous feature of the 540-acre site is the beech pollards, some of which are almost 500 years old. There is a programme of regular free walks and talks. Given the wood's accessibility (just north of Junction 6 of the M4), it would be the perfect place to get away from it all if it were not for the fact that every year half a million other people have the same idea! / Times: pedestrians 24 hours; vehicles 08.00-one hour after sunset; Rail: Slough (then bus to Farnham Common).

Bushy Park, Middx
0181-979 1586   off map
This ancient deer park was part of Wren's grand design for neighbouring Hampton Court. Herds of red and fallow deer roam its 1,100 acres. The Woodland Gardens, with their fine azaleas, camellias and rhododendrons, are a post-war addition and make a nice place for a picnic. They boast a fine chestnut avenue which is the focal point of Chestnut Sunday – a traditional Victorian parade and picnic, takes place on the second Sunday in May. / Times: 06.30-00.00; Rail: Hampton Wick.

Chelsea Harbour SW10
0171-351 4433   3–4B
This contemporary riverside development, with its attractive marina, makes a pleasant place for a riverside walk on a sunny day and has some good views. Given its relatively central location, the harbour has a surprisingly far-away feel. / Tube: Earl's Court (then C3 bus).

Chiswick House * W4
Burlington Lane   0181-995 5390   1–3A
The mainly wooded, 64-acre gardens of this fine neo-classical villa have suitably Italianate highlights – statues, temples, urns and obelisks – and there is also a lake and a cascade waterfall. There is a picnic area. The house (to which there is an entry charge) is run by English Heritage. / Times: park 08.00-dusk; information centre 08.30-30 minutes before the park closes; Tube: Turnham Green (then E3 bus); Café.

Crane Park Island, Middx
Crane Park, Twickenham   0171-278 6612   off map
This small island (just over four acres), reached by bridge is believed to have been where Guy Fawkes obtained his supplies of gunpowder. Nowadays, the attractions are more peaceful and it's an agreeable site, run by the London Wildlife Trust. There are three paths, one of which (the Hobbin Path) is suitable for disabled people. In the summer school holidays there is a play-scheme – call for details. / Times: 24 hours; Rail: Whitton.

Gunnersbury Triangle Nature Reserve W4
Chiswick   0181-747 3881   1–3A
This six-acre site developed a rich covering of vegetation after being surrounded by railway tracks in the late c19. It is now managed by the London Wildlife Trust. During school summer holidays there is a usually a full-time warden and a programme of free events. / Times: Tue 10.00-16.00, Fri & Sun 14.00-16.30; also some Sats & school hols; Tube: Chiswick Park.

Hampton Court Palace *, Middx
0181-781 9500   off map
The wonderful garden and the park of Wolsey's great riverside palace are open to the public without charge. Around the gardens, in the 560-acre park, graze the descendants of the deer hunted by the Tudor monarchs. There is a charge for access to the Palace. / Times: 07.00-21.00 (dusk if earlier); Rail: Hampton Court; Café.

Holland Park W8
Ilchester Place   0171-602 9483   1–3B
Until some 40 years ago, Holland Park was an extraordinary hangover from former days – a private 'country' estate of 52 acres, in the middle of London. It maintains a unique and charming character. Apart from its superb formal gardens, it benefits from the Kyoto Garden, installed by Japanese benefactors in 1991, and an area of woodland. Other attractions include a large adventure playground and the Ecology Centre. The Park contains the Orangery and the Ice House (see also). / Times: 07.30-30 mins before dusk; Tube: Holland Park, Kensington High Street.

Hyde Park W2
0171-298 2000   3–1C
The greatest of the central Royal Parks was originally acquired by Henry VIII as a private hunting ground. Its 340 acres now offer a variety of attractions, ranging from the formal gardens along its south side, Rotten Row (a bridleway for more than 300 years), a river (the Serpentine) and areas of woods and grass. In the summer there are concerts at the bandstand. Speakers' Corner (see also) is situated in the north-east corner of the park. / Times: 05.00-00.00; Tube: Knightsbridge, Hyde Park Corner, Marble Arch, Lancaster Gate.

Kensington Gardens W8
0171-298 2100   3–1B
The private gardens of Kensington Palace, laid out in 1728, were opened to the public by Queen Victoria. Attractions in the 275 acres include the Boating Pond (model boats only, please), the charming small statue of Peter Pan and the very pretty area in the immediate vicinity of the Palace itself.). In summer there are regular concerts and entertainments. / Times: dawn-dusk; Tube: Bayswater, Lancaster Gate, Queensway, High Street Kensington; Café.

Marble Hill House *, Middx

Richmond Rd, Twickenham   0181-892 5115   off map

Built in the 1720s, this Palladian villa – one of the most perfect surviving examples of the type – inhabits a large park which stretches down to the river. There is an admission charge for the house but the grounds are free.
/ Times: dawn-dusk; Tube: Richmond; Café.

Osterley Park *, Middx

Isleworth   0181-560 3918   off map

This great c18 house is set in 140 acres of landscaped park and farmland with ornamental lakes. There is a charge for admission to the house and for car parking but not for entry to the grounds. / Times: park, 09.00-19.30 or sunset if earlier; Tube: Osterley.

Pet Cemetery W2

Hyde Park (near Victoria Gate)   0171-298 2112   1–2B

Originally a garden in which family pets and pets of friends of the houseowner were buried, this site was later given as a cemetery, and by 1903, when it closed, there were 300 graves. At the moment, individuals and schools can visit free though there is a charge for group tours. / Times: by appointment; Tube: Queensway, Lancaster Gate.

Portobello Road Market W10, W11

1–2B

On Saturday, the market is undoubtedly the place in west London to combine people-watching and browsing. It stretches for over a mile, and in fact comprises several different markets of which the most famous, antiques, is at the south end. / Tube: Notting Hill Gate, Ladbroke Grove.

Ranelagh Gardens SW3

Royal Hospital Rd   3–3D

Apart from when they are cordoned off every year for the famous Chelsea Flower Show (in May), these well-kept gardens lead a rather low-profile life. They are, however, unusually pretty and intimate. Don't miss the neighbouring Royal Hospital (see also). / Times: 10.00 (Sun 14.00)-30 mins before dusk, but closed 13.00-14.00; Tube: Sloane Square.

Riverside Walk

See the South section for suggestions of interesting walks by the Thames.

Ruislip Woods, Middx

Ruislip   01895-250635   off map

These 700 acres include, in the 250-acre Park Wood, the largest unbroken area of woodland in London. A short guide to Ruislip Woods is available in local libraries or from the Recreation Unit, Local Services, Civic Centre, Uxbridge, Middx UB8 1UW. / Times: woodland centre Sat & Sun 12.00-15.30; Tube: Ruislip (then 331 bus); Café.

North London

Introduction

North London's unique strength is the way it contains pockets of real nature, which seem to be only a stone's throw from the metropolis itself. The most obvious example is **Hampstead Heath**, but there is also **Highgate Wood** (which you can reach on foot using the **Parkland Walk**), and both are within a few tube-stops of anywhere in central London.

In addition, much of North London is provided with fine parks. It has its own ornamental Royal Park, in the form of **Regent's Park**. Its extension, **Primrose Hill**, has exceptional views and the northerly **Alexandra Palace Park** gives yet another fine perspective on the city below. The grounds of **Golder's Green Crematorium** are a fine amenity relatively unknown to those outside the locality.

Few would dispute that Hampstead is by far the finest village in London and two of its lovely period houses may be visited – **Burgh House** (whose museum gives the history of the area) and **Keats House**. The village's grandest residence, **Kenwood House**, at the top of the Heath, has a major art collection.

In a very different idiom, the **Saatchi Gallery** in St John's Wood brings some of the most challenging contemporary art before the public.

For people who like being among people, the undoubted attraction here is **Camden Market**.

For children, the green spaces and the nature are probably the main plus points. For the more inquisitive, however, the **Wellcome Galleries**, with their interactive displays, should not be overlooked.

Islington Visitor Information Centre N1
44 Duncan St   0171-278 8787   4–3D
/ Times: Mon 14.00-17.00, Tue-Fri 10.00-17.00, Sat 10.00-13.30 & 14.30-17.00; Tube: Angel.

Harrow Tourist Information Centre, Middx
The Civic Centre, Station Rd, Harrow
0181-424 1103   off map
/ Times: Mon-Fri 09.00-17.00; Rail: Harrow & Wealdstone.

Indoor attractions

Barnet Museum, Herts
31 Wood St, Barnet   0181-440 8066   off map
*This local history museum covers archaeology to costume.
Artefacts in the collection include banners from the Battle of
Barnet – the penultimate battle in the Wars of the Roses.*
/ Times: Tue-Thu 14.30-16.30, Sat 10.00-12.00 & 14.30-16.30; Tube: Barnet
(then 1/2 mile walk or 184 bus).

Bruce Castle Museum N17
Lordship Lane   0181-808 8772   off map
*Haringey's local museum occupies an elegant and striking
Tudor house which contains a wide collection of items of local
interest, from the Highgate Roman kiln through to Victorian
costumes. Roland Hill, the inventor of the penny post, was
taught by his schoolmaster-father here and a postal history
collection reflects his connection with the house. Temporary
art exhibitions are held from time to time, and during the
summer, there are regular arts and crafts activities.*
/ Times: Wed-Sun 13.00-17.00; Tube: Wood Green, then 243 bus.

Burgh House NW3
New End Square   0171-431 0144   4–1A
*This handsome Queen Anne house (1703) is well-worth a
visit for its architecture, its pictures and its creaking charm.
The ground floor is used as a community centre and houses
temporary art exhibitions. The museum is on the first floor
and has displays and objects about the history of Hampstead
(which has long been regarded as one of the most desirable
places to live in or near the capital) and changing exhibitions
on the history of the area. The house makes an ideal
stopping-off point between the tube station and the Heath.*
/ Times: Wed-Sun (and Bank Hols) 12.00-17.00; Tube: Hampstead; Café.

Camden Arts Centre NW3
Arkwright Rd   0171-435 2643   4–2A
*The Centre's three galleries hold about half a dozen
contemporary art exhibitions a year. During shows, there are
usually artist-led Sunday talks every two to three weeks.*
/ Times: Tue-Thu 11.00-19.00, Fri-Sun 11.00-17.30; Tube: Finchley Road.

Church Farmhouse Museum NW4
Greyhound Hill   0181-203 0130   off map
*Built in 1660, this charming building (the oldest hereabouts)
combines permanent displays of c19 life – a period dining
room (but with panelling dating from c17), scullery (done out
as a laundry complete with a display of smoothing irons) and
kitchen (with c17 hearth) – with changing exhibitions about
local and social history and decorative arts and crafts.*
/ Times: Mon-Thu 10.00-12.30 & 13.30-17.00, Sat 10.00-13.00
&14.00-17.30, Sun 14.00-17.30; Tube: Hendon Central.

Crafts Council N1
44a Pentonville Rd   0171-278 7700   4–3D
The Council is the national body for promoting contemporary crafts, such as pottery, textiles and printing. Its premises include picture and reference libraries as well as a gallery. There are five major exhibitions a year. An information service relating to contemporary British crafts is available by phone or letter as well as to visitors. / Times: Tue-Sat 11.00-18.00, Sun 14.00-18.00; Tube: Angel; Café.

Estorick Foundation * N1
Northumberland Lodge, 39A Canonbury Square
0171-704 9522   4–2D
A new museum, in a listed Georgian building, showing works from the collection of modern Italian art collected by Eric and Salome Estorick. It is particularly known for its Futurist works, including Balla, Severini and Russolo, but there are also paintings, drawings and sculptures from artists such as Modigliani, Sironi and Campigli, and oils by de Chirico. / Times: Tue 11.00-18.00; Tube: Highbury & Islington; Café.

Forty Hall, Middx
Forty Hill, Enfield   0181-363 8196   off map
Forty Hall was first built in 1629. It has since had a chequered history and been owned by many families (the last being the Parker Bowles family who lived there until the '40s). Its attractions are the richness and diversity of the interiors and the extensive grounds (suitable for picnicking). In use as a museum for the last four decades, the hall now houses a display on local history, a popular children's gallery (with gas mask, toys and school items all from the '40s), an exhibition devoted to advertising and packaging and a gallery with monthly-changing art exhibitions. / Times: Thu-Sun 11.00-17.00; Rail: Enfield Town (then 191 or 231 bus); Café.

Glasshouse N1
21 St Albans Place   0171-359 8162   4–3D
You are welcome to stop by at this Islington glass-blowing workshop, where you can watch intricate glass artefacts being blown and formed. There's also a gallery, in which you can see impressive examples, all for sale, of course. / Times: Tue-Fri 10.00-18.00; gallery, Sat 10.00-17.00; Tube: Angel.

Grange Museum of Community History NW10
Neasden Lane   0181-452 8311   1–1A
Brent's community museum, in a converted c18 stable block, includes an Edwardian draper's shop (transplanted from Willesden High Road) and a Victorian Parlour. A permanent exhibition, The Brent People, includes a computerised database of local photographs. This is a child-friendly museum, with a ball pool for under fives and an enclosed garden (with Victorian herb border) open for picnicking. New from 1997 is an exhibition on local Jewish life. / Times: Jun-Aug, Tue-Fri 11.00-17.00, Sat 10.00-17.00, Sun 14.00-17.00; Sep-May, Mon-Fri 11.00-17.00, Sat 10.00-17.00; Tube: Neasden.

Harrow Museum and Heritage Centre, Middx
Headstone Manor, Pinner View, Harrow
0181-861 2626   off map
Built for the Archbishops of Canterbury in the c14,
this moated manor house has '30s interiors which are
in the course of renovation. It benefits from a pretty setting
in a park, and there is also a large and interesting tithe
barn (where a Victorian room setting, changing exhibitions
and local history displays are on view). / Times: Wed-Fri
12.30-17.00, other days, call to check); Tube: Harrow-on-the-Hill
(then H14 or H15 bus); Café.

Islington Museum Gallery N1
268 Upper St, Islington   0171-354 9442   4–2D
It is surprising that Islington, which has undergone a
transformation from notorious slum to 'in' part of the capital,
lacks a fully-fledged local museum. However, this building is
the setting for between eight and ten exhibitions relating to
the area annually, including history, sociology, ethnic culture
and arts and crafts, and is a 'start'. It is hoped it is the
precursor to a more permanent and comprehensive venture
for the millennium. / Times: Wed-Sat 11.00-17.00, Sun 14.00-16.00;
Tube: Highbury & Islington.

John Perry Wallpapers N1
Cole and Son Wallpapers, 142-144 Offord Rd
0171-607 3844   4–2D
TV companies go to this Islington concern for period
wallpaper for historic sets such as Pride and Prejudice. The
wall coverings for the Houses of Parliament and Buckingham
Palace also originate here. Established in 1875, the company
continues to hand-print all its papers using traditional block
methods. It can take weeks to print a single roll – fortunately,
groups can see several stages of production in one visit!
/ Times: by appointment; Tube: Highbury & Islington.

Keats House NW3
Keats Grove   0171-435 2062   4–1A
The great poet spent most of his adult life in this Hampstead
house (consisting of two very pretty Regency cottages), which
contains memorabilia of Keats and his family. / Times: Apr-Oct,
10.00-13.00 (not Sun), 14.00-18.00 (Sat & Sun 17.00); Nov-Mar, 13.00
(Sat & Sun 14.00)-17.00 & also Sat 10.00-13.00; Tube: Hampstead.

Kenwood House NW3
Hampstead Lane   0181-348 1286   4–1A
Perching like a grand wedding cake above Hampstead Heath,
this neo-classical house (with Robert Adam façade, 1760s)
provides a great cultural climax to a visit to the heath. The
house (which was bequeathed to the nation by the first
Earl of Iveagh in 1927) is certainly worth a view (the library is
reckoned as one of Adam's finest rooms), as are the artistic
treasures within, which include a Rembrandt self-portrait and
Vermeer's Guitar Player. / Times: Apr-Sep 10.00-18.00, Oct-Mar
10.00-16.00; Tube: Archway or Golders Green (then 210 bus); Café.

Lauderdale House Community Arts Centre N6

Waterlow Park, Highgate Hill   0181-348 8716   1–1C

*The two galleries of the Elizabethan house in the centre of
the attractive Waterlow Park hold frequently changing
exhibitions. Entry to the house and galleries are free except
when special exhibitions are being held. Call before you travel.*
/ Times: Tue-Fri 11.00-16.00; Tube: Archway (then 143, 210 or 271 bus);
Café.

Museum of Domestic Architecture and Design N11

Middlesex University, Bounds Green Rd
0181-362 5244   off map

*The core of the six collections is the Silver Studio – one of the
leading independent design studios from the 1880s until the
1950s. The collection includes wallpaper and textile designs.
Also of note: the Sir J M Richards Library; the Peggy Angus
Archive; the Sir Charles Hasler Collection; the Crown
Wallpaper Archive and the British and Domestic Design
Collection 1850-1950.* / Times: admission by (telephone)
appointment, Mon-Fri 10.00-16.00; Rail: Bowes Park, New Southgate
Tube, Bounds Green; Café.

Old Speech Room Gallery, Harrow School, Middx

Church Hill, Harrow-on-the-Hill
0181-869 1205   off map

*This famous school has accumulated a number of treasures
over the years. There is a nucleus of antiquities plus a series
of temporary exhibitions which draw on highlights of the
collection, such as c19 watercolours and printed books.*
/ Times: 14.30-17.00 (not Wed); school holidays, hours vary;
Tube: Harrow-on-the-Hill (then 258 bus).

Saatchi Collection * NW8

98A Boundary Rd   0171-624 8299   4–3A

*This white 'space' in St John's Wood affords a striking setting
in which to display a changing selection of items from
advertising magnate Charles Saatchi's collection of modern
art, which is almost certainly the finest of its type in the UK.*
/ Times: Thu 12.00-18.00; Tube: St John's Wood, Swiss Cottage,
Kilburn High Road.

Stephens Collection N3

Avenue House, East End Rd, Finchley
0181-346 6337   off map

*In 1918, Henry Charles Stephens bequeathed Avenue House
and its grounds to the public. (Stephens Senior was the
inventor of the famous blue-black writing fluid still used for
marriage registers.) Since 1993, Avenue House has housed a
collection of artefacts relating to ink and ink products. The
collection includes original enamel signs, quill and steel-nibbed
pens.* / Times: Tue, Wed & Thu 14.00-16.30; Tube: Finchley Central.

Wellcome Building NW1

183 Euston Rd   0171-611 8727   4–4C

There are two interesting attractions in the Wellcome Trust's august HQ building, near Euston. 'Science for Life' is a permanent exhibition, featuring a wide range of displays, many of which benefit from the application of the latest interactive technology – it includes a human cell, magnified a million times, through which you can walk. The 'History of Medicine' gallery principally draws on the huge collection of the Wellcome Institute Library. A new building at 210 Euston Road is a gallery housing a programme of changing temporary exhibitions. / Times: Mon-Fri 09.45-17.00, Sat 09.45-13.00 (not 210 Euston Road); Tube: Euston, Euston Square, Warren Street.

Outdoor attractions

Abney Park Cemetery N16

Stoke Newington High St

0181-806 1826, visitor centre 0171-275 7557   1–1C

A surprisingly country-like place (it was originally laid out as an arboretum), this cemetery took over (around 1840) from Bunhill Fields as the final resting place of London's dissenters and non-conformists. The main entrance has been restored and there is a visitor centre which has information boards covering the geology of the stones of the site, the history and the (mainly local) characters buried here. / Times: summer 09.00-19.00, winter 09.00-15.00; visitor centre, generally 10.00-16.00; Rail: Stoke Newington.

Alexandra Palace N22

Alexandra Palace Way   0181-365 2121   off map

This 200-acre North London park is made special by its panoramic views over the metropolis. The popular Grove Shows have been running for a decade and offer live music every Sunday afternoon between June and August and, during school holidays, high quality performances for kids. Permanent attractions include a children's playground, an animal enclosure (with llama, pony, donkeys and deer) and a conservation area (near the Wood Green entrance). There is also a gallery/shop with a changing display of fine art (Mon-Sat 10.00-17.00, Sun 10.30-16.30). / Times: 24 hours; Tube: Wood Green, then W3 bus.

Camden Lock NW1

0171-284 2084   4–2B

Occupying renovated warehouses, this is arguably the more 'grown up' part of Camden Market. Fashions, jewellery, books, antiques – are among the enormous variety of things available from the stalls and shops. The lock is open all week, but, as with the rest of the market, Saturday and Sunday are the peak time for a visit. There are frequent summer attractions (generally during the week), such as street theatre, music and art shows. / Times: 09.30-18.00; Tube: Camden Town, Chalk Farm; Café.

Camden Market NW1
Camden High St (and surrounding area)   4–2B
At the weekend, the whole of hip young London seems to descend on Camden for its markets. By no means are prices particularly bargain basement, though, and unless you are shopping for the latest in 'wicked' style, the real point of the trip is to stroll around window-shopping and people-watching.
/ Times: Thu-Sun 09.00-17.00; Tube: Camden Town.

Camley Street Natural Park NW1
12 Camley St   0171-833 2311   4–3C
In the heart of King's Cross, on Regent's Canal (though not accessible from it), this community nature reserve houses a variety of wildlife habitats include a marsh, pond and a wood. There is an on-going educational programme and a variety of children's events take place year-round – call for details. Donations appreciated. / Times: Mon-Thu 09.00-17.00; Sat & Sun in summer 11.00-17.00, in winter 10.00-16.00; Tube: King's Cross.

Coldfall Wood N10
Crichton Avenue   0181-348 6005   off map
These 35 acres of ancient woodland to the north of Muswell Hill are of great ecological interest and you can see examples of the returning fashion for traditional coppice management. If you intend to explore, call the Conservation Officer who can provide you with further information, and the leaflet, Historic Woodlands in Haringey. / Tube: East Finchley.

Finsbury Park N4
0181-880 9138   4–1D
A large part of the 115 acres of this Victorian park is taken up with various sports facilities (for which there is generally a charge), and a boating lake, so there's often a lot of activity. For information about kids' and other activities call the Finsbury Park Action Group 0181-802 2612.
/ Times: dawn-dusk; Tube: Manor House, Finsbury Park; Café.

Freightliners Farm N7
Sheringham Rd   0171-609 0467   4–2D
This 3 1/2 acre city farm in Islington is among the oldest in London. It has all the usual farm animals, but a less common attraction is a sensory garden for disabled people. From 1998 the Farm will host the Sheep and Wool Fair on the second Bank Holiday in May where the attractions will include sheep dog trials, sheep shearing demonstrations, different types of sheep and country crafts. / Times: Tue-Sun 09.00-13.00 & 14.00-17.00; Tube: Highbury & Islington, Holloway Road.

Fryent Country Park NW9
Fryent Way, Kingsbury   0181-900 5653   1–1A
For those in search of real country in the town, the 260 acres of unspoilt rural farmland here, sandwiched between Wembley and Kingsbury, are pretty much the perfect answer. Nature walks, ponds and a wildlife area are among the attractions. / Times: 24 hours; Tube: Kingsbury, Wembley Park.

Gladstone Park NW10
Dollis Hill Lane   1–1A
*William Gladstone was a frequent visitor to the fine house
(1824) which forms the centrepiece of this very varied
90-acre park between Neasden and Willesden. Other
attractions include an arboretum filled with hundreds of exotic
trees from all over the world, a pond with ducks and geese,
and an old walled garden.* / Times: 08.00-dusk; Tube: Neasden,
Dollis Hill.

Golder's Green Crematorium NW11
Hoop Lane   0181-455 2374   1–1B
*For the casual observer, spring (when 100,000 crocuses
bloom) is the time to visit the only purpose-built crematorium
in London, set in 13 1/2 acres of landscaped grounds.
Founded in 1902, the building features northern Italianate
architecture (by Sir Ernest George, RA, who also designed
Claridge's Hotel). Those cremated here include Marc Bolan,
Joyce Grenfell, Gustave Holst, Charles Rennie Mackintosh,
Sigmund Freud, Ronnie Scott and Peter Cook.*
/ Times: 09.00-19.00 (winter 17.00); Tube: Golders Green; Café.

Hampstead and Highgate Ponds NW3
Hampstead Heath
0181-348 9945/0171-485 4491   4–1A
*Hampstead Heath boasts three places to swim. During the
season (first Sat before the May Bank Holiday to the third
Sun in Sep) you can choose between the Hampstead Pond
(mixed), the Highgate Pond (men) and the Kenwood Pond
(women). All ponds limit children to those aged eight and
over, and to one per adult. The pools are not well signposted,
so don't forget your map.* / Times: summer, mixed 07.00-19.00, single
sex 07.00-21.00 (or sunset if earlier); winter, call; Tube: Hampstead, Kentish
Town (then 214 or C2 bus).

Hampstead Heath NW3
0181-348 9945/0171-485 4491   4–1A
*Hampstead Heath's 791 acres, presided over by the City of
London, offer everything from a fine c18 house and art
collection with formal gardens – Kenwood (see also) – to
heathland which is as close as you get to real countryside
near central London. There are also tremendous vistas over
the metropolis. Other attractions include concerts at the
bandstand on Golders and Parliament Hills and talks and
walks. For kids there is a playpark, and a programme of free
entertainment including Punch and Judy, magicians and
clowns. A full diary of events is available with an A5 SAE
from The Parliament Hill Staff Yard, Highgate Road, London
NW5 1PL.* / Times: 24 hours; Tube: Hampstead, Golders Green.

North London

Highgate Wood N6
Muswell Hill Rd   0181-444 6129   off map
The 70 acres of Highgate Wood were taken over by the Corporation of London as "an open space for ever" in 1886. There's a small playground and a sports ground, but the attraction is essentially what the name suggests – an ancient woodland, with diverse flora and fauna, all just a few yards from the Archway Road. If you're planning to spend more than an hour or so in the wood collect or send for a copy of the free, attractively illustrated booklet, Highgate Wood, which lists the flora, birds and butterflies which can be spotted there. This, a newsletter and other leaflets on the local natural history are available with an A5 SAE from Corporation of London, Highgate Wood, Muswell Hill Road, London N10 3JN. You might also like to explore the neighbouring 48-acre Queen's Wood (across the Muswell Hill Road), which is relatively wild and boasts an equally impressive selection of wildlife. / Times: 07.30-dusk; Tube: Highgate.

Parkland Walk N22, N8, N4
0181-348 6005
Walking down a railway track might seem a rather hazardous activity, but the redundant line between Finsbury Park station and Alexandra Palace is actually a Local Nature Reserve and offers an interesting alternative for a country walk in town, separated by Queens and Highgate Woods (see also). The total length of the walk is 4 1/2 miles, and it takes around two hours. It is worth getting the free leaflet (which includes a map, available from the Haringey Conservation Officer on the number given) to avoid getting lost in Highgate Wood or giving up when faced with the very unpark-like Archway Road. / Tube: Finsbury Park (south section); Highgate (middle); Alexandra Palace, rail or W3 bus back to Finsbury Park (north).

Parliament Hill Lido * NW3
Gordon House Rd   0171-485 3873   4–1B
One of London's three remaining lidos, built in 1936, this unheated, open-air pool is open from the first weekend in May to mid-September. It is free only for two hours every morning. / Times: Mon-Sun 07.00-09.00; Rail: Gospel Oak.

Primrose Hill NW3
0171-486 7905   4–3B
The hill – the 61-acre continuation of Regent's Park to the north – is the most central natural vantage point over London, and is therefore justly celebrated for its views. When there's enough snow, it's an extremely atmospheric place to go tobogganing. There has been an outdoor gymnasium on the site since Victorian times and there are still 20 types of exercise equipment available for year-round use. To get you in the mood, the walk along the towpath of the Regent's Canal from Camden Lock or Little Venice is a nice way of approaching (or leaving) the hill. / Times: 24 hours; Tube: Chalk Farm, Camden Town.

Queen's Park NW6

Kingswood Avenue   0181-969 5661   1–2B

*This 30-acre Kilburn park has been owned and run by the
Corporation of London since 1886. It's not particularly large,
but popular in this relatively under-provided part of town. It's
an especially good park for children, with its large, supervised
playground and a paddling pool. There is also an ornamental
garden and a fine, Victorian bandstand. The second Sunday in
September sees the annual community entertainment day –
involving music, comedy and games – which draws big
crowds.* / Times: 07.00-dusk; Tube: Queen's Park.

Railway Fields N4

(Opposite Haringey/Green Lanes Station)
0181-348 6005   1–1C

*This conservation park, in a former British Rail goods coal
yard, has been developed for teaching primary school children
about nature. There is a meadow, a woodland and a pond,
and even a unique hybrid plant – the Haringey Knotweed.
A visitor centre, with leaflets, provides information about the
ecology of the site (as well as other places of environmental
interest in the borough).* / Times: Mon-Fri 10.00-17.00 (phone to
confirm); Tube: Manor House.

Regent's Canal Towpath

*The canal's eight or so miles run from the docks in the east,
through Camden at Camden Lock, along the north of the
Park and on to the waterway's conclusion in Paddington
(where it meets the Grand Union Canal). There is a towpath
along the entire length. The prettiest part is towards its
western conclusion in the stretch through Little Venice W9.
For the leaflet Explore London's Canals, which also covers
walks on the Grand Union Canal, send an SAE and £1 to
British Waterways (London Canals), Toll House, Delamere
Terrace, Little Venice, London W2 6ND.* / Camden Town
(eastern end), Paddington (west), Warwick Avenue (Little Venice).

Regent's Park NW1
0171-486 7905   4–3B

Regent's Park's 297 acres have an atmosphere all of their own, perhaps because the park was, in fact, designed as a grand garden suburb. In the end, only eight of the 26 villas which Nash planned at the beginning of the last century were built (though a few more have recently been added). Queen Mary's Gardens have one of the finest selections of blooms in the country and the lake boasts an impressive variety of wildfowl. The annual Music Village (early July) is Britain's longest-running "festival of living traditions from around the world" and is a platform for international popular music, dance and crafts. During the summer, music is performed on a regular basis, at the bandstand or at various other points around the park at weekends and some evenings during the week. There are also children's workshops during school holidays. / Times: 05.00-30 mins before dusk; Tube: Regent's Park, Baker Street, Camden Town, Great Portland Street.

Roundwood Park NW10
Robson Avenue, Harlesden Rd   1–2A

A fine 60-acre Victorian park in Willesden that has impressive floral displays and an aviary stocked with exotic birds. There is also a children's playground. / Times: 08.00-dusk; Tube: Willesden Green.

Waterlow Park N6
Highgate Park   1–1C

Given to the public by Sir Sydney Waterlow in 1889, this "garden for the gardenless" is situated on a steep hillside and has an unusual three-level lake, formal gardens and terraces. Lauderdale House (see also) is within the park. Facilities include a children's play area. / Times: 07.30-dusk; Tube: Highgate.

South London

Introduction

South London boasts many of the best free destinations, especially for a family day out.

Just over Chelsea Bridge, **Battersea Park** is the only one of the central parks to benefit from a river frontage, and offers a wide range of attractions. A little further south, **Dulwich Park** is very fine (and, on Friday, can be combined with a visit to the **Dulwich Picture Gallery**). **Crystal Palace Park** also makes an interesting destination (especially on a Sunday or a Bank Holiday afternoon, when the Museum is open).

To the south east, **Greenwich**, with **Greenwich Park**, the **Royal Naval College** and the **Old Royal Observatory**, makes an excellent destination, and the **Thames Barrier** is not far away.

To the south west, Richmond, and the adjoining **Richmond Park** is also a very attractive place for a full day's exploration (especially bearing in mind the attractions around Twickenham, just on the other side of the river – see West).

If you're heading back to central London from some of the more grown-up cultural attractions south of the river, such as the **Imperial War Museum**, it's worth bearing in mind that the early evening sees some of London's best free music at the **National Theatre** (early evenings, weekdays; lunchtime, Saturday) and the **Royal Festival Hall** (lunchtimes, Wed-Sun; early Friday evening).

Greenwich Tourist Information Centre SE10
46 Greenwich Church St   0181-858 6376   1–3D
/ Times: May-Oct 10.15-16.45; Nov-Apr Mon-Thu 11.00-13.00 & 13.45-16.00, Fri-Sun 10.15-16.45; Rail: Greenwich.

Lewisham Tourist Information Centre SE13
199-201 Lewisham High St   0181-297 8317   1–4D
/ Times: Mon-Fri 09.00 (Mon 10.00)-17.00; Rail: Lewisham.

Richmond Tourist Information Centre, Surrey
The Old Town Hall, Whittaker Avenue, Richmond
0181-940 9125   off map
/ Times: Mon-Fri 10.00-18.00, Sat 10.00-17.00, Sun (May-Oct) 10.15-16.15; Tube: Richmond.

Croydon Tourist Information Centre, Surrey
Katharine St   0181-253 1009
/ *Times: Mon-Wed & Fri 09.00-18.00, Thu 09.30-18.00, Sat 09.00-17.00;*
Rail: East or West Croydon.

Indoor attractions

Addington Palace, Surrey
Gravel Hill, Croydon   0181-654 4404   off map
The Palace – home in its day to six archbishops of Canterbury
– was built in 1776 for Barlow Tregothick, Lord Mayor of
London. It is set in a 'Capability' Brown landscape and is of
interest for its architecture and history. Parts of the Palace
were restored in 1900 by Norman Shaw and the décor of
some rooms dates from then. The Great Hall is lined with
polished Italian walnut and the impressive fireplace is made
from Istrian marble. Now a conference and banqueting suite,
the palace is open about eight days a year for guided tours,
and to societies on additional days by arrangement. / *Times:*
see text; Rail: East Croydon then 130 bus; Café.

Age Exchange Reminiscence Centre SE3
11 Blackheath Village   0181-318 9105   1–4D
The highlight here is the charming '30s 'general shop' with its
genuine fittings and original stock. This "hands-on museum of
the 1930s and 1940s" should interest anyone who can
remember those days, as well as those who cannot. There is a
changing temporary exhibition at the rear. The café serves
tea and cakes in period style, in the garden in fine weather.
/ *Times: Mon-Sat 10.00-17.00; Rail: Blackheath; Café.*

Avery Hill Winter Garden SE9
Avery Hill Park, Avery Hill Rd   0181-316 8991   off map
Bananas grow in south London! There is also a fine collection
of cacti in this imposing domed glasshouse, originally built as
a private winter garden by one Colonel North (who died in
1900). There are cold, temperate and semi-tropical houses.
/ *Times: 10.00-12.00 & 13.00-16.00; Rail: Falconwood.*

Battersea Arts Centre * SW11
Lavender Hill   0171-223 6557   1–4B
The gallery of this busy arts centre, housed in Battersea's fine
former Town Hall, holds regularly changing exhibitions. There
is generally a charge for the other attractions but it's worth
picking up one of the monthly calendars to look out for the
occasional free event. / *Times: Mon 10.00-18.00, Tue-Sat 10.00-22.00,*
Sun 16.00-22.00; Rail: Clapham Junction.

Bethlem Royal Hospital Archives & Museum, Kent

Monks Orchard Rd, Beckenham
0181-776 4307/4227   off map
Founded in 1247, the original 'Bedlam' is home to many paintings and drawings by artists who have suffered mental disorder. The Museum is closed for around a year from the end of August '97 – many key exhibits being 'on tour' to celebrate the 750th anniversary of the founding of the Hospital. / Times: museum Mon-Fri 9.30-17.00 (not Bank Hols) but best to check in advance; archives by appointment; Rail: Eden Park, or East Croydon (latter then 119, 166, 194, or 198 bus).

Bexley Museum, Kent

Hall Place, Bourne Rd, Bexley   01322-526574   off map
The building is part Tudor and part Jacobean and is set in extensive gardens and among nurseries. The museum contains permanent displays of local geology, natural history and archaeology, plus a mock-up of a Victorian bathroom! There are varied temporary exhibitions, mostly on a local history theme. / Times: Mon-Sat 10.00-17.00, Sunday 14.00-18.00 (summer); Rail: Bexley; Café.

Black Cultural Museum SW9

378 Coldharbour Lane   0171-738 4591   1–4C
Every aspect of the history of black people in Britain is covered by the collections of this Brixton museum. There are also changing exhibitions and displays of work by black artists. / Times: Mon-Sat 10.30-18.00; Tube: Brixton.

Blewcoat School SW1

23 Caxton St   0171-222 2877   2–4C
In 1709, local brewer William Green paid for the building of this single room. The aim was to provide an education for poor children and it was used as a school until 1926. Bought by the National Trust in 1954, restored in 1975, it is now the Trust's London Information Centre. / Times: Mon-Fri 10.00-17.30; Tube: St James's Park.

Bromley Museum, Kent

The Priory, Church Hill, Orpington
01689-873826   off map
This local history museum is housed in a largely medieval building and is set in attractive gardens. Exhibitions include "archaeology of the borough till Domesday", a social history gallery and a programme of varied temporary exhibitions. One highlight is Bromley's first fire engine which dates from the early c19 and a display commemorating Sir John Lubbock, the first Lord Avebury (1834–1913), whom we have to thank for Bank Holidays. There is a programme of temporary exhibitions throughout the year. / Times: Apr-Oct incl Bank Hols, Sun-Fri 13.00-15.00, Sat 10.00-17.00; Nov-Mar closed Sun and Bank Hols; Rail: Orpington; Café.

Crystal Palace Museum SE19
Anerley Hill   0181-676 0700   off map
The Museum tells the story of the Crystal Palace, erected in Hyde Park as a temporary structure for the Great Exhibition of 1851. The glass building attracted much interest and was bought and moved to Upper Norwood where it stood until it burned down in 1936. The museum is housed in a brick-built part of the original structure. Exhibits are mainly photographs, including pictures of the fire, as well as some Victorian souvenirs. The museum is set in 200 acres of parkland – see also Crystal Palace Park. / Times: Sun & Bank Hol Mon 11.00-17.00; Rail: Crystal Palace.

Cuming Museum SE17
155-157 Walworth Rd   0171-701 1342   1–3C
Southwark is one of the most historically interesting parts of London. Its museum (just south of the Elephant and Castle) has a rather unusual basis, being derived largely from the objects collected by the Cuming family between 1786 and 1902. It includes a dynamo built by Faraday, ships in bottles and 'curses' such as a cow's heart with nails through it. There are often temporary exhibitions. Occasionally, there are early evening talks, which may be on a wide range of topics. The summer holidays usually see special events for the children. / Times: Tue-Sat 10.00-17.00; Tube: Elephant & Castle.

Dulwich Picture Gallery * SE21
College Rd   0181-693 5254
recorded information 0181-693 8000   1–4C
This is the oldest public art gallery in the UK (1814) and was designed by Sir John Soane. It is almost as notable for its neo-classical design as for its important collection of old masters, which includes works by Rembrandt, Van Dyck, Claude and Poussin. There is a particularly good selection of c17 Dutch art and also some of the greatest portraits by Gainsborough and Reynolds. Perhaps because its scale is not at all intimidating, this is one of the most enjoyable galleries to visit and the building has great atmosphere. A curiosity at its centre is the mausoleum, which contains sarcophagi of the museum's founders. Combine a visit here with one to Dulwich Park (see also), opposite. / Times: Fri 10.00-17.00; Rail: North or West Dulwich; summer tea tent.

Eltham Palace SE9
Tilt Yard Approach, Court Rd   0181-294 2548   off map
Both Henry VIII and Elizabeth I spent much of their childhood here – a place which has belonged to the Crown since 1305. Only the Great Hall, with its impressive hammer-beam roof remains, but it is an interesting site, approached over London's oldest bridge, dating from the c15. The elevated location affords good views over London. / Times: Thu, Fri & Sun 10.00-18.00 until Oct '97, thereafter call to check; Rail: Eltham; Café.

Erith Museum, Kent
Erith Library, Walnut Tree Rd, Erith
01322-336582   off map
*This small museum, on the second floor of Erith Library,
features displays of local history, with an Edwardian kitchen
and displays about the River Thames. The exhibits relating to
local industries are being updated during 1997.*
/ Times: Mon, Wed & Sat 14.15-17.15 (Sat 17.00); Rail: Erith.

George Inn SE1
77 Borough High St   0171-407 2056   5–4C
*The only remaining galleried coaching inn in London is c17 in
origin and was mentioned by Dickens in* Little Dorritt. *It is
still a public house (leased by the National Trust to
Whitbread) and so anyone can go and have a look at its
interior. Parts are extremely characterful and include the
tavern clock which dates back to 1745. Around 20.00 on the
first Monday of the month (not Bank Hols) a group plays
traditional English music. / Times: Mon-Sat 11.00-23.00,*
Sun 12.00-15.00 & 19.00-22.30; Tube: London Bridge.

Greenwich Borough Museum SE18
232 Plumstead High St   0181-855 3240   off map
*The permanent displays at this local museum (housed on the
upper floor of Plumstead Library) concentrate on local
geology, archaeology and wildlife – it seems the fox and the
badger displays are particularly popular with younger visitors.
Children's activities are organised on Saturdays, and during
school holidays. / Times: Mon 14.00-19.00; Tue & Thu-Sat 10.00-13.00 &
14.00-17.00; Rail: Plumstead.*

Honeywood Heritage Centre *, Surrey
Honeywood Walk, Carshalton   0181-773 4555   off map
*This c17 house is free only on three days a year: the first
Sunday in December and for the Heritage Open Weekend
(mid-September, with free tours of the house and gardens).
When you do get in you'll find an exhibition setting out the
history of the borough (Sutton), including an audiovisual
display. / Times: call for details; Rail: Carshalton; Café.*

Horniman Museum SE23
London Rd   0181-699 1872   1–4D
*'Free Museum' is carved in stone at the entrance of this
fascinating Forest Hill museum (adjacent to delightful, very
well-maintained gardens boasting a bandstand and lovely
views over London). A visit here has something for everyone.
The building grew out of the enthusiasms of Victorian tea
magnate Frederick Horniman, who in 1897 opened this art
nouveau gallery to house his collection of natural history
exhibits and musical instruments. There are now many
fascinating, very well-structured exhibits, the aquarium being
particularly enjoyable. There is a good programme of talks
and workshops in the museum, and music in the bandstand.
/ Times: Mon-Sat 10.30-17.30, Sun 14.00-17.30; Rail: Forest Hill.*

Imperial War Museum * SE1
Lambeth Rd   0171-416 5000
recorded information 0891-600140   2–4D
Despite its macho image, which the guns outside the entrance do nothing to dispel, this venue puts on such a variety of displays every visitor will find something of interest. There is, of course, the fine collection of planes, tanks and every imaginable weapon of war. Using inter-active video technology, the museum also stages some spectacular exhibits including reconstructions such as the WWI Trench, and WWII Blitz Experiences, complete with sounds and smells. Exhibits go far beyond the 'hardware' of war. Some tell the human side of the story, for example, the new permanent VCGC (Victoria Cross, George Cross) Gallery displays medals and relates the stories of the people who won them. Note: the Museum is in the final stage of redevelopment – call to check the exhibition you want to see will be open on the day you plan to visit. / Times: 16.30-18.00; Tube: Lambeth North (closed till end July '97), Elephant & Castle; Café.

Kingston Museum, Surrey
Wheatfield Way, Kingston upon Thames
0181-546 5386   off map
This purpose-built Edwardian museum houses two major exhibitions: Ancient Origins, which illustrates the borough's past from pre-history to Anglo-Saxon times, and the Eadweard Muybridge Gallery. The latter is named after the local Victorian pioneer of cinematography who proved that trotting horses do have all four hooves off the ground at one time. Highlights of the displays include the original Zoopraxiscope and a panorama of San Francisco from 1878. A new gallery, Town of Kings, opens in late 1997 and will continue the story of Kingston-upon-Thames from the Saxon period to the present. / Times: Mon, Tue & Thu-Sat 10.00-17.00; Rail: Kingston.

Little Holland House, Surrey
40 Beeches Avenue, Carshalton
0181-770 4781   off map
The Grade II listed interior is the main (but not the sole) attraction of this former home of artist, designer and craftsman, Frank Dickinson (1874-1961). Wanting to create a house that would meet with the approval of his mentors, John Ruskin and William Morris, he designed and built the house, with contents, himself. Highlights include the painted frieze in the master bedroom, the carved timbers of the living room and the decorated fireplace surrounds. / Times: 1st Sun of month, Bank Hols and preceding Sun (except Jan) 13.30-17.30; Rail: Carshalton Beeches.

Livesey Museum SE15

682 Old Kent Rd   0171-639 5604   off map

Southwark's museum for children presents a lively and varied programme of 'hands-on' exhibitions. They are principally directed at the under-12s, but parents and other minders are welcome to take part. There is a picnic area. / Times: Tue-Sat 10.00-17.00; Tube: Elephant & Castle (then 53 or 172 bus).

London Glass Blowing Workshop SE1

7 Leathermarket, Weston St   0171-403 2800   5–4C

The Glass Art Gallery at this well-established glassblowing studio has been recently refurbished and enlarged. In addition to visiting the three or four exhibitions a year you can watch the handblown molten glass being blown and formed. If you so wish, you can, of course, buy the products on the way out. / Times: Mon-Fri 10.00-17.00; Tube: London Bridge, Borough; Café.

Merton Heritage Centre, Surrey

The Canons, Madeira Rd, Mitcham

0181-640 9387   off map

Located in a c17 mansion house in Mitcham, the Centre tells the story of the borough of Merton and its people, past and present. There is a changing programme of exhibitions and special events. Displays usually include photographic material, artefacts, videos and a 'hands-on' section. / Times: Fri & Sat 10.00-17.00 (other times by appointment); Rail: Mitcham then 270, 280, or 355 bus to Mitcham Cricketers or Vestry Hall; (or tube to Morden then 118 bus to Vestry Hall; tube to Raynes Park then 152 bus to Mitcham Fair Green); Café.

Mounted Police Museum, Surrey

Mounted Training Establishment,

Imber Court, East Molesey   off map

Horses are trained here for public duty and ceremonies, and to get to the museum you pass through the stables. The small collection contains artefacts relating to the mounted branch since 1920 – there are paintings, documents, flags and regalia. Note that the staff are on police duty and visits may have to be cancelled or curtailed. / Times: by (written) appointment, groups and clubs preferred; Rail: Thames Ditton.

Museum of Artillery in the Rotunda SE18

Repository Rd, Woolwich   0181-316 5402   off map

A fine museum, housed in a quite extraordinary Nash building. It began life as a huge replica bell tent, used as a marquee in the grounds of the Prince Regent's home at Carlton House, and was relocated to its present site in 1819. The wide-ranging collection within illustrates the development of artillery from its beginnings to the present day (and, includes, for example, parts of the Iraqi 'supergun'). The museum is due to move to Woolwich Arsenal before the millennium. / Times: Mon-Fri 13.00-16.00 (not Bank Hols); Rail: Woolwich Arsenal.

Museum of Garden History SE1
Lambeth Palace Rd   0171-261 1891   2–4D
*A replica c17 century garden is one of the attractions of this
South Bank museum, attractively housed in a former church.
Exhibits explain the history of gardening, and there is a large
collection of historic gardening tools and other items. Other
points of interest include the graves of the two John
Tradescants, gardeners to Charleses I and II, and the final
resting place of Captain Bligh of HMS Bounty! / Times: Sun-Fri
10.30-16.00 (Sun 17.00); Tube: Waterloo, Victoria (then 507 bus,
Sun C10 bus); Café.*

Oxo Tower SE1
Barge House St   0171-401 3610   5–3A
*The free public viewing platform from the eighth floor of this
South Bank art deco landmark, a former power generating
station, offers excellent views, especially across the river to the
City and St Paul's. The building itself is home to the retail
studios of artisans such as jewellers, artists, furniture makers
and ceramicists. The nearby park is a good place for children
to let off steam and you could picnic on the benches on the
Thames-side promenade between here and the Royal
Festival Hall. / Times: studios Tue-Sun 11.00-18.00; restaurants & bars till
late; Tube: Waterloo, Blackfriars, (from October '98, Southwark); Café.*

Photofusion SW9
17A Electric Lane   0171-738 5774   1–4C
*This Brixton gallery has monthly-changing shows by leading
photographers. / Times: Tue-Fri 10.30-17.30, Sat 12.00-16.00;
Tube: Brixton.*

Police Traffic Museum SE6
South East Traffic Unit, Catford Garage,
34 Aitken Rd   1–4D
*All the artefacts in this small museum are connected with
traffic patrol. The collection includes vehicles from the '60s
through to the '80s and related books. Note that staff are on
duty and can be called away at short notice or visits cancelled
if operations so require. / Times: by (written) appointment, groups and
clubs preferred; Rail: Bellingham.*

Public Record Office, Kew
Ruskin Avenue, Kew, Surrey, TW9
0181-392 5200   1–3A
*This is the national archive of England and Wales, and the 96
miles of shelving holds records created or acquired by central
government and the central courts of law from the c11 until
the present day. All the original public records, previously held
at Chancery Lane, are now housed at Kew, and this is where
you find, for example, the Domesday Book, Jane Austen's will
and Guy Fawkes's confessions. It is envisaged that a museum
will open at some point during 1998. / Times: Mon & Wed-Sat
09.30-17.00 (Thu 19.00), Tue 10.00-19.00; closed Bank Hol weekends,
public holidays and much of Dec; Rail: Kew Bridge (or tube/rail to
Kew Gardens).*

Pumphouse Educational Museum SE16

Lavender Pond Nature Park, Lavender Rd
0171-231 2976   1–3D

*Formerly the building housed dock machinery, now it is home
to the Rotherhithe Heritage Museum and is surrounded by a
nature park and pond. The museum traces the story of
Rotherhithe and its people as told by objects found on the
foreshore of the Thames during 12 years beachcombing by
local man, Ron Goode. The Nature Park has trails through an
orchard, herb gardens and past the 'minibeast city'. Reed
beds fringe the pond which is frequented by heron, swan,
tufted duck and dragonflies.* / Times: Mon-Fri 09.30-15.00;
Tube: Rotherhithe.

Puppet Centre Trust SW11

BAC, Lavender Hill   0171-228 5335   1–4B

*The Trust's fine collection of puppets date from Victorian
times to the present. There are also rare photographs, slides,
posters and memorabilia. The Library is open for research
and contains videos as well as books.* / Times: Mon-Fri 14.00-18.00;
Rail: Clapham Junction; Café.

Royal British Legion Poppy Factory, Surrey

20 Petersham Rd, Richmond   0181-940 3305   1–4A

*Each year around 34 million poppies are made here, as is the
wreath the Queen lays at the Cenotaph on Remembrance
Sunday. The factory was set up in 1922, originally in south
east London, to help ex-members of the armed forces who
are disabled but who can work to continue to be gainfully
employed. Individuals and groups are welcome to join a tour
around this working factory and find out more about the
history of the business.* / Times: by appointment Mon-Thu 10.00 and
13.30; Tube: Richmond.

The Royal Festival Hall * SE1
0171-960 4242   2–3D

The concert hall at the centre of Europe's largest cultural complex offers an extensive range of free foyer events, all of which are set out in the centre's colourful monthly programme. There's almost always something on Wed-Sun, 12.30-14.00, usually music and often of high quality, in addition to the regular Commuter Jazz, Fri 17.15-18.45. During the summer, there is the Great Outdoors series of events on the river terraces and sometimes even on the roof. The annual three-week Ballroom Blitz, is an opportunity to have a go at almost any type of dancing. There are workshops during the day while the events in the evening range from ceilidhs to '70s disco dancing. The extravaganza culminates in a ballroom day. While you're visiting the centre, you can take in one of the ever-changing exhibitions in the Festival Hall Galleries, which are open all day and evening. If you visit the RFH towards the end of the day, the view across the Thames from the upper terrace is one of the finest in London. Afterwards, you might consider taking in the foyer music at 18.00 at the nearby National Theatre (see also). / Times: 10.00-22.30; Tube: Embankment, Waterloo; Café.

The Royal National Theatre * SE1
South Bank   0171-633 0880   2–3D

Its uncompromising exterior may have taken a while to win Londoners' affections, but the interior of Sir Denys Lasdun's riverside building has always found favour with theatre-goers. Even if you're not going to a show, you can still explore the various levels of the intriguing layout and view one or more of the several exhibitions, which are open all day every day (except Sunday). Or take in the music – it might be early or contemporary, classical, folk or jazz – at 18.00 nightly and 13.00 on Saturdays. / Times: Mon-Sat 10.00-23.00; Tube: Embankment, Waterloo; Café.

Royal Naval College SE10
King William Walk, Greenwich   0181-858 2154   1–3D

Wren's baroque Greenwich Hospital (for retired sailors) became the Royal Naval College in 1873. The extraordinary Painted Hall (whose entire interior is decorated with paintings by Sir James Thornhill) should not be missed, and the attractive c18 chapel (decorated by Athenian Stuart) is also worth a visit. / Times: Mon-Sun 14.30-17.00 (last admission 16.30); Rail: Greenwich.

Museum of the Royal Pharmaceutical Society of Great Britain SE1

1 Lambeth High St   0171-735 9141   2–4D
The museum traces five centuries' history of medicinal drugs and their use in Britain. It looks at the scientists and traders who invented, developed and sold the potions and pills, and the patients who swallowed them and whose blood fed the leeches. Changing displays show the rapid development of our understanding of the human body in the c19 and c20 and the impact of new drug therapy on today's society. Non-members must make a (telephone) appointment with the Curator for a guided tour. / Times: by appointment, Mon-Fri 09.00-13.00 & 14.00-17.00; not public hols; Tube: Vauxhall, Lambeth North.

Shirley Windmill, Surrey

Upper Shirley Rd, Croydon   0181-656 6037   off map
This five-storey brick tower mill was built in 1859. It retains skeleton sails, its fantail and a Kentish cap. It last worked in 1892, but restoration is scheduled to be completed by the end of 1997. Note that due to the number and steepness of the stairs the mill is not suitable for the very young or for those who are less than fit. / Times: 1st Sun in month from National Mills Day (early May), 1st Sun in Oct; Rail: East Croydon then 130 bus; Café.

South London Art Gallery SE15

65 Peckham Rd   0171-703 6120   1–3D
This elegant Victorian gallery was re-opened in 1993. It shares its site with the well-known Camberwell College of Arts. The gallery presents a changing programme of innovative contemporary works by international artists. / Times: Tue, Wed & Fri 11.00-18.00, Thu 11.00-19.00, Sat & Sun 14.00-18.00; Rail: Peckham Rye, or by 36 bus from Victoria, or 12,171 or P3 bus from Elephant & Castle.

Southwark Cathedral SE1

Montague Close   0171-407 2939   5–4C
In origin c13 (but with many later alterations), this fine building, just over London Bridge, is a hidden gem. Being rather overshadowed by the fame of the cathedrals on the other side of the river, it benefits from an absence of crowds. This is, in fact, the oldest Gothic church in London (and was apparently the inspiration for Westminster Abbey). Nor does it want for historical associations – the Bard's brother, Edmund Shakespeare was buried here in 1607, and that same year saw the baptism of university founder John Harvard. At 13.10 there is an organ recital on Monday and an instrumental music recital on Tuesday. (For information on the exhibitions and special events, call 0171-407 3708.) / Times: Mon-Fri 07.30 (Sat & Sun 08.30)-18.00; Tube: London Bridge; Café.

Tate Gallery of Modern Art Visitor Centre SE1
Bankside Power Station, 25 Sumner St
0171-887 8000   5–3B
Until Spring 2000 (when the Tate Gallery of Modern Art is scheduled to open), a small Visitor Centre provides information about the new Gallery. It shows architectural plans and details of the conversion of this former power station, designed by Sir Giles Gilbert Scott (who was also responsible for red telephone boxes). The plans for the new gallery show that the chimney (which was limited to 325ft to be lower than the dome of St Paul's, opposite) is being retained, probably as a viewing tower. / Times: Wed 12.00-19.00; Tube: Blackfriars, Waterloo, from Sept 1998 Southwark.

Wandsworth Museum SW18
The Courthouse, 11 Garratt Lane
(opposite the Arndale Centre)   0181-871 7074   1–4B
This local history museum tells the story of Wandsworth from prehistoric times to the present day. There are year-round temporary exhibitions, and also worksheets, competitions and holiday activities for children. Highlights are the fossilised skull of a woolly rhino (found under Battersea Power Station), a reconstruction of a wartime shelter and a re-creation of a Victorian parlour. / Times: Tue-Sat 10.00-17.00 (Sun 14.00); Rail: Wandsworth, East Putney (then 37 or 337 bus).

Wimbledon Society's Museum SW19
22 Ridgway, Wimbledon   0181-296 9914   1–4B
This small, voluntarily run museum depicts the history of Wimbledon from prehistory to the present day and includes archive material. Until recently, of course, Wimbledon was at a good remove from the metropolis, and its rural past is well illustrated by the collection of watercolours, photographs and prints. Highlights are scale models of local manor houses which no longer exist. / Times: May-Oct, Sat & Sun 14.30-17.00; Nov-Apr, Sat 14.30-17.00; Tube: Wimbledon, Putney Bridge then 93 bus.

Woodlands Art Gallery SE3
90 Mycenae Rd   0181-858 5847   off map
This Georgian house has a great artistic tradition. It was built for John Julius Angerstein (the "father of the Lloyds insurance market"), whose extraordinary accumulation of paintings was, after his death, acquired by the government to form the basis of the National Gallery's collection. Woodlands now presents exhibitions of contemporary art (often by well-known artists) which change every month. The building, situated in a pretty garden, is shared with the local history library (closed Wed and Fri; tel 0181-858 4631), through whose exhibits visitors are welcome to browse. / Times: Mon, Tue & Thu-Sat 11.00-17.00; Sun 14.00-17.00; Rail: Westcombe Park.

Outdoor attractions

Battersea Park SW11

Albert Bridge Rd   0181-871 7530   3–4D

This 200-acre park is one of the most popular, most central family destinations, and rightly so as it's full of things to look at and do – events are publicised on noticeboards. The long river frontage (punctuated by the Peace Pagoda given to the people of London in 1985 by a Japanese Buddhist Order) has lovely views across the river to Chelsea and the Royal Hospital. Other attractions include the Pump House art gallery, a herb garden, a deer enclosure and London's largest adventure playground for five to 16 year olds. Excellent literature is available from the Park Office (to the left of the Albert Bridge entrance), including Introducing Battersea Park which has a map, and well produced tree and nature trail brochures. There is also a zoo for which there is a small charge. / Times: 08.00-dusk; Tube: Sloane Square (then 19 or 137 bus); Café.

Bermondsey Antiques Market SE1

Bermondsey Square   1–3C

If you arrive at dawn, you'll have missed the best bargains at London's largest antiques market (so take a torch and dress warmly). As the sun rises, the professionals depart and the trippers take over. / Times: Fri 05.00 (or earlier)-13.00; Tube: Night buses N53 (from Trafalgar Square), or later: Borough, Elephant & Castle; Café.

Blackheath SE3

1–4D

For centuries the heath was wild and a popular haunt for highwaymen. Now, however, this large, flat expanse of grass which separates the pretty village of Blackheath from Greenwich Park is well-known for its annual Kite Festival (see Regular Events). A couple of pools (one a boating pond) aside, generally its attraction is as a big, open space for running about on. A visit here would combine well with one to the Age Exchange Reminiscence Centre (see also). / Rail: Blackheath.

Brixton Market SW9

Brixton Station Rd   1–4C

The characterful warren of streets and alleys around Brixton tube station houses as exotic a market as you will find in London, with food and fabrics from Africa, the Caribbean and elsewhere, as well as the mundane items you expect to find anywhere. / Times: Mon-Sat 08.00-17.30 (Wed 13.00); Tube: Brixton; Café.

Chumleigh Gardens SE5

Chumleigh St, Burgess Park   0171-525 1050   1–3C
*Tucked away behind high walls in the bland expanses of
Burgess Park is a collection of erstwhile almshouses (from
1821) and a new multi-cultural garden. The garden is divided
into areas: Afro-Caribbean, English, Islamic, Mediterranean
and Oriental, and all flora is labelled. There are two ponds,
one of which is surrounded by striking blue tiles. Due to the
water, and the poisonous or spiny nature of some of the
plants, kids should not be allowed to explore unaccompanied.*
/ Times: Tue, Thu & Sun 14.00-16.00 (other times by arrangement);
Tube: Elephant and Castle then P3, 185, 176 or 40 bus (or rail to Denmark
Hill, then 42 bus); Café and picnic area.

Crystal Palace Park SE19

Sydenham   0181-778 7148   off map
*The Crystal Palace was an enormous glasshouse which served
as a hall at the Great Exhibition before being dismantled and
moved to Sydenham, where it was consumed by fire in 1936.
There's a small museum about it (see also). However,
there is much more to this large and attractive park than just
historical associations. The permanent free attractions include
a maze, a children's play area and a unique collection of
Victorian full-scale models of dinosaurs. Regular events
include the Victorian Day (last weekend in June). Over the
May Day Bank Holiday there is also a vintage car rally.
During the Easter and summer school holidays there are
special events for kids, some of which are free. Year-round
you can follow the Tree Trail, and details about this and other
events, can be obtained from the Information Centre (at the
Penge entrance) on the number above.* / Times: 07.00-dusk,
information centre 09.00-17.00; Rail: Crystal Palace.

Deen City Farm SW19

39 Windsor Avenue, Merton Abbey
0181-543 5300   off map
*Animals at this five-acre city farm range from the expected
(cows, sheep and pigs, including a goat and a pony) to rare
breeds, and there is also an expanding pure breed poultry
programme. The emphasis is on seeing and touching, and
there are also information boards, and, at weekends,
demonstrations of crafts such as spinning. A shop and café
sell the farm's own fresh produce. Donations are appreciated.*
/ Times: Tue-Sun 09.00-17.30; school hols Mon-Sun; Rail: Raynes Park (then
200 bus to Haslemere Avenue); Café.

Dulwich Park SE21

College Rd   0171-525 1554   1–4C

A fine collection of trees is the particular attraction of this fine 75-acre Victorian park. The rhododendrons and azaleas are a feature and for these May is the time to visit. The Park Ranger service (0181-693 5737) organises walks, for example bat-spotting on summer evenings, and talks throughout the year, and produces a quarterly events programme. The neighbouring Belair Park, of 30 acres, is relatively little known, but worth looking at having been laid out in the late c18, in the classic English landscape style. You can combine a visit to both with a trip to the Dulwich Picture Gallery (see also) or the Horniman Museum (see also). / Times: 08.00-dusk; Rail: North or West Dulwich.

Green Chain Walk

The Green Chain Walks are a twisting network of over 15 miles of well-signposted routes. They link many of south east London's fine parks and open spaces into walks which contain as much greenery as possible. Four leaflets detailing the walks (Thamesmead or Erith to Oxleas Wood; Thames Barrier to Oxleas Wood; Oxleas Wood to Mottingham; and Mottingham to Crystal Palace or Chislehurst Common) are available from South East London libraries and Tourist Information Centres.

Greenwich Markets SE10

1–3D

If you enjoy nosing around market stalls, it's well worth making a special weekend journey to Greenwich, which has what is possibly the most comprehensive – as well as the most attractively situated – series of marketplaces in London. The individual markets are: Bosun's Yard (crafts), Greenwich Church Street; the Antiques Market, Greenwich High Road; the Central Market (general), Stockwell Street; and the Craft Market – the original market (1837) formerly a collection of fruit and veg stalls but now selling arts and crafts. / Times: Sat & Sun 09.00-17.00, summer sometimes Fri; Rail: Greenwich; Café.

Greenwich Park SE10
0181-858 2608 1–3D
These 183 acres, enclosed in 1433, constitute the oldest of London's Royal Parks and was popular with Henry VIII who was born locally and who held jousting tournaments here every year. It is one of the best outdoor venues offering something to entertain all the family. There are red and fallow deer in the deer park that has been here since the c15 and, of course, flower gardens and a children's playground. Brass bands play at the bandstand on Sunday afternoons and evenings during the summer, on some August afternoons and evenings there are performances of Shakespeare's plays (picnicking by the audience is encouraged), and there are family days in May and July. There is also a free summer soccer school during school holidays (0181-850 2866). The view from the top of the hill by the Old Royal Observatory (see also) is quite something and don't miss the Information Centre (at the St Mary's Gate entrance) which has rooms explaining the history and wildlife of the park.
/ Times: dawn-dusk; Rail: Greenwich; Café.

Ham House *, Surrey
Ham, Richmond   0181-940 1950   off map
There is a charge for admission to this outstanding Stuart house, which has been restored and reopened by the National Trust. Admission to the interesting garden – c17 in origin and in the process of restoration to a very formal layout – is, however, free of charge. / Times: Sat-Thu 10.30-18.00 (or dusk, if earlier); Tube: Richmond (then 65 or 371 bus).

Lesnes Abbey Woods, Kent
Lesnes Abbey Rd, Belvedere   0181-312 9717   off map
Taking its name from the c12 abbey whose remains still stand, this 200-acre wood, together with the adjoining Bostall Heath and woods (160 acres), makes up one of the largest areas of trees in south London. The spring sees a tremendous show of wild daffodils, and then wood anemones and bluebells. A rather unusual attraction is the natural fossil bed, in which the public can search for shark and ray teeth, and shells. The woods are quite hilly and it's a good idea to take stout footwear. / Rail: Abbey Wood.

Morden Hall Park SM4
Morden Hall Rd, Morden   0181-648 1845   off map
This informal 125-acre park, owned by the National Trust, was laid out around 1860 as a deer park. It is given additional interest by a complex network of waterways coming off the River Wandle (which were designed to be partly ornamental and partly to power snuff mills, whose buildings still stand). You can also visit the craft workshops and watch local artists and artisans at work. / Times: dawn-18.00; craft workshops 10.00-17.00, daily not Tue; Tube: Morden; Café.

South London

Old Royal Observatory * SE10
Greenwich Park   1–3D
*You can bestride two hemispheres at the top of the hill in
Greenwich Park. There's a charge to go inside the charming
c17 Observatory (which has one of London's few surviving
Wren interiors), but the 0 degree line is marked outside as
well. Many people consider that being photographed with one
foot in the western hemisphere, and the other in the eastern,
is an obligatory souvenir. The Observatory is the spiritual
home of the Greenwich Time Signal. A longer-established
visual sign of time passing is the red ball on top of the
Observatory, which descends its pole at 13.00 every day –
its original purpose was to enable seafarers to set their
chronometers correctly. The view from outside the
Observatory is possibly the best in London and also
summarises the history of London. Immediately ahead, you
see the city's imperial past (the Royal Naval College), to the
West sprawls the City and central London, and, across the
river, looms what is perhaps the future – Canary Wharf.*
/ Times: dawn to dusk; Rail: Greenwich.

Oxleas Woods SE10
*One of the capital's last remaining ancient woodlands (some
8,000 years old) and only quite recently saved from the
road-builder's bulldozer. The wood supports over 33 species
of tree and shrub, including the rare wild service tree, the
hornbeam and guelder rose. Fungi proliferate, with more than
200 species, including the 'story-book' toadstool (red with
white spots), the poisonous fly agaric. The wood forms part of
the Green Chain Walk (see also). There is parking within the
woods, accessible from Shooters Hill (A207) and some of the
other surrounding roads.* / Rail: Falconwood.

Richmond Park, Surrey
0181-948 3209   1–4A
*This enormous park (2,500 acres) was created by Charles I
by enclosing farmlands, and in 1625 he moved the court here
to escape the Plague. It has changed little in the last 300
years, and still contains some 700 red and fallow deer.
Because it has been little disturbed, the park offers some rare
natural habitats and has been declared a Site of Special
Scientific Interest. The Isabella Plantation (towards the
Kingston Gate) is noted for its fabulous collection of azaleas,
and views from King Henry's Mound (which may have been a
bronze age barrow) stretch as far as the City.* / Times: pedestrians
24 hours; vehicles dawn-30 mins before dusk; Tube: Richmond.

Riverside walk

Arguably the finest walking in London, and certainly some of its best vistas, can be enjoyed on the mostly continuous paths which run along the Thames, on both the north and south banks from Kingston in the west to Docklands in the east.

The south bank is on balance the better place to walk, because it is generally more peaceful and also because, almost invariably, the north bank is the more picturesque to look at. If you get bored, the distances between bridges are quite short so you can always swap sides.

The most rural-feeling of the more central stretches of the river is the (muddy) towpath on the south bank between Putney Bridge and Barnes Bridge. Hammersmith, with its numerous pubs, makes a good stopping-off point on such a walk.

If it's a stroll in the centre of town you are after, there is a continuous fine stretch of river between the Houses of Parliament and Tower Bridge. Head eastwards and you get a magnificent vista of St Paul's. Along Victoria Embankment (north bank), and later in the City, the walk is continuous and leads to the picturesque Tower of London and St Katherine's Dock (see also).

On the same stretch of river, one of the nicest routes, not least because it is away from the traffic, is along the south side between the South Bank Centre and Westminster Bridge. Again there are magnificent views (especially, if you are walking west of the Houses of Parliament) and it is a particularly nice walk at night. One of the best views in London is from the footbridge built into Hungerford railway bridge (between Embankment Tube and the South Bank Centre). For a fine view of Tower Bridge visit the up and coming area of Bermondsey, east of the bridge, near the Design Museum.

If you wander even further east, you cross a narrow footbridge where Fagin hanged himself in Oliver. The warehouses here have yet to be yuppified and it is particularly atmospheric on a darkish day when the water has been replaced by smooth mud. On the promenade at Cherry Wharf are three life-sized statues: a girl, a cat and an old man. These figures comprise Mr Salter's Daydream, as explained by a plaque on the site.

Other walks to consider are a stroll along the riverside path in Battersea Park, the north bank to the east of Kew bridge, and, further out of town, the extremely pretty stretch at Richmond.

Surrey Docks Farm * SE16
Rotherhithe St   0171-231 1010   1–3D
This well-equipped city farm is in a slightly away-from-it-all picturesque location, on the banks of the Thames opposite Canary Wharf. Attractions include an orchard, a blacksmith's forge, a herb garden, beehives and a bee room – it is possible in the autumn for kids to help collect the honey. Family visits are free but there is a charge for groups. / Times: Tue-Fri 10.00-17.00, Sat & Sun 10.00-13.00, 14.00-17.00; school hols closed Mon-Fri 13.00-14.00; Tube: Rotherhithe; Café.

Thames Barrier * SE18
1 Unity Way   0181-854 1373   off map
The Thames Barrier is the largest movable anti-flooding protection device in the world – it was built in response to the ever-greater threat posed to low-lying central London by high tides (which have been rising at the rate of about 75cm a century). It spans the 520m Woolwich reach and consists of 10 separate, massive, movable steel gates. The most spectacular time to visit is during the annual all-day test (in September or October), when the entire barrier blocks the high tide, but it's an impressive sight at any time. (There are also monthly closures but these happen as early in the morning as possible to minimise closure of the river.) There is a charge for the visitors centre, but not for access to the riverside walk or the children's play area. / Rail: Charlton.

Vauxhall City Farm SE11
24 St Oswald's Place   0171-582 4204   1–3C
It may be less than an acre in size, but this tiny farm, run on a voluntary basis, boasts a full range of farm animals. Look out for rabbits, geese, ponies, donkeys and sheep. You can even (at a cost) have riding lessons. / Times: Sun 10.30-17.00; Tube: Vauxhall; Café sometimes, Sun 14.00-16.00.

Wimbledon Common SW19
0181-788 7655   1–4B
The common extends to nearly two square miles, some of which is quite rough countryside and there are several ponds with much birdlife. It is the setting for one of London's few remaining windmills, which now houses a museum (Apr-Oct) about the history of this type of machinery, complete with working models, for which there is a charge, albeit a small one. / Times: pedestrians 24 hours; vehicles sunrise-sunset; Tube: Southfields; Café.

Woolwich Foot Tunnel
North Woolwich Pier, Ferry Approach
0181-854 888 ext 5493 (to check lift times)   off map
Another chance to walk under the Thames which (see also Greenwich Foot Tunnel) combines nicely with a trip over the river, on the Woolwich Free Ferry (see also). / Times: lift Mon-Sat 07.30-18.00, Sun 09.00-16.00; tunnel 24 hours unless there is major maintenance work; Rail: north of the Thames, North Woolwich; south of the Thames 180 bus to Greenwich then 188 bus to Euston, etc.

The City

Introduction

The tiny but very wealthy Square Mile is often likened to a city-state. It has its own ways of doing things which have been arrived at over practically a millennium of running its own affairs, and its long history has left it rich in historic buildings and institutions. Its wealth and importance are symbolised by its medieval **Guildhall**, where great state banquets are often held, and by the great cathedral of St Paul's. Its other great sights include the **Tower of London**, **Tower Bridge** and the **Monument**.

Trading and, later, banking were the foundations of the City's wealth. Today more international banks gather together in the City than anywhere else. Sadly, most trading and banking business nowadays happens over the telephone – the Stock Exchange, as a trading place, is no more. For the casual visitor, the **Bank of England Museum** provides the only insight into these sadly now rather closed worlds. If you want to see institutions at work, the barristers' **Inns of Court** are some of the most interesting, picturesque and immutable of all – and most are open to the public to a greater or lesser extent.

The City also has indoor attractions, such as the **National Postal Museum**, and, on its fringes, the **Mount Pleasant Sorting Office** and the **London Silver Vaults** – all of which should be of interest to older children and adults.

If planning a visit, it's a good idea to arrive in the late morning and begin by visiting the City of London Information Centre – there is usually at least one free lunchtime concert in one of the City's fine churches (many by Wren).

City of London Information Centre EC4
St Paul's Churchyard   0171-332 1456   5–2B
The City has a conveniently positioned general tourist information centre right by St Paul's. It has copies of City Events, *an excellent guide to the musical and other events happening in the City during that month. / Times: Apr-Sep: Mon-Sun 09.30-17.00; Oct-Mar: Mon-Fri 09.30-17.00, Sat 09.30-12.00; Tube: St Paul's.*

Liverpool Street Station Tourist Information Centre EC2
5–2D
The office is in the approach to the Underground station. / Times: Mon-Sat 08.00-18.00, Sun 08.30-17.00; Tube: Liverpool Street.

Indoor attractions

Bank of England Museum EC2
Bartholomew Lane   0171-601 5545   5–2C
Housed within the forbidding building of the Bank itself, the museum is at the very centre of the City of London and traces the history of the Bank from its royal foundation in 1694 to the present. There are interactive videos to bring the institution's activities to life. Curiosities include documents relating to George Washington (a former customer) and to Kenneth Grahame (a former Secretary of the Bank, and the author of The Wind in the Willows*). / Times: Mon-Fri 10.00-17.00, Sat, Sun & Bank Hols 11.00-17.00 (summer); also day of the Lord Mayor's Show (2nd Sat in Nov) see also; Tube: Bank.*

Barbican * EC2
Silk St   0171-638 4141   5–1B
Love it or hate it, the City's sprawling, concrete arts and residential complex is impressive with its vast concert hall, theatre, cinema and sweeping internal spaces – the biggest arts centre under a single roof anywhere in the world. There is free music in the foyer (anything from jazz to Irish folk) most days 17.30-19.15 (and also most Suns 12.30-14.30) – see the Centre's programme for details – and there are often special theme events on Bank Holiday weekends. / Times: 09.00 (Sun 12.00)-23.00; Library Mon & Wed-Fri, 09.30-17.30, Tue 09.30-19.30; Concourse Gallery Mon-Sat 10.00-19.30; Sun & Bank Hols 12.00-19.30; Tube: Barbican, Moorgate; Café.

Chartered Insurance Institute EC2
20 Aldermanbury   0171-417 4425   5–2C
The Institute's characterful building (near the Guildhall) houses displays illustrating the history of insurance through the ages. The main hallway (not generally accessible to the public) houses the world's largest collection of firemarks – the signs which, in earlier times, indicated a building was insured, and by whom. However, there is also a small museum that tells the history of insurance and houses an old fire engine. The building dates from the 1930s and, ironically, it was the only building in the area that wasn't bombed in the Blitz. It's a good idea to phone before you set out. / Times: Mon-Fri 09.00-17.00; Tube: St Paul's.

The Clerks' Well EC1
14-16 Farringdon Ln   0171-619 7994   5–1A
The source that gave the surrounding area of Clerkenwell its name was subsequently filled in and built over. The well chamber can still be visited – you can see an iron pump and plaque from 1800, c16 refacing work and a later wall probably from the c17. Access is by key from the local library, see details below. Groups – 4-15 people – preferred. / Times: Mon, Tue & Thu, by appointment with the attendant from Finsbury Public Library, 245 St John Street, EC1, 0171-619 7994; Mon-Thu 09.00-20.00, (Tue & Sat 17.00, Fri 13.00); Tube: Farringdon, Angel, Barbican.

Clockmakers' Company Collection EC2

Guildhall Library, Aldermanbury   0171-332 1868   5–2C

The Clockmakers' clock collection dates from the c14. This single-room museum contains a glittering and fascinating selection of timepieces, including curiosities such as the first electric clock and one powered by gas. There is also a large silver watch reputed to have belonged to Mary Queen of Scots. To hear the collection at its best make sure you are there at noon. / Times: Mon-Fri 09.30-16.45; Tube: St Paul's.

College of Arms EC4

Queen Victoria St   0171-248 2762   5–3B

The College is the body empowered by the sovereign to determine everything relating to the granting and bearing of coats of arms. The main part of its building is c17, while the impressive wrought iron gates came from a country house and were given by an American benefactor. The Earl Marshal's Court Room is one of the finest, secular, period rooms in the City to which the public has access. / Times: Mon-Fri 10.00-16.00; Tube: Blackfriars.

Family Record Centre (formerly part of the Public Record Office) EC1

1 Myddleton St   0181-392 5300   5–1A

If you want to trace your family history, you can now find microfilms of census, probate wills and non-conformist registers (formerly at Chancery Lane) and Birth, Marriage and Death Registers (previously at St Catherine's House) on one site in Islington. To visit the reading rooms you need a document such as a driving licence or cheque card with your signature on it, or if you are not British, your passport or national identity card. / Times: Mon & Wed-Fri 09.00-17.00, Tue 10.00-19.00, Thu 9.00-19.00, Sat 09.30-17.00; closed Bank Hol weekends and public holidays; Tube: Farringdon, Angel.

Guildhall EC1

Gresham St   0171-606 3030   5–2C

The hall on this site has been the most important secular building in the City since the c11 – many important events and glittering state banquets take place here. Much of the present building (which is on a spectacular scale) dates from 1440, and, although fire and bomb damage have taken their toll, a fair amount of the original remains. The magnificent hall is usually open to casual visitors (ring to check), but pre-booked parties (10–50 people) may also visit the Old Library and the medieval crypt. / Times: May-Sep Mon-Sun 10.00-17.00; Oct-Apr closed Sun; Tube: St Paul's, Bank, Moorgate.

Guildhall Library EC2

Aldermanbury   0171-332 1868   5–2C

This elegant library specialises in the history of London. If this is an area which interests you, this is a delightful place to while away a couple of hours. There is an area where visitors can consume packed lunches. / Times: Mon-Sat 9.30-17.00 (restricted service Sat); Tube: Moorgate, Bank, St Paul's.

Livery Halls
*The proud and ancient livery companies of the City boast a
large number of halls some of which are extremely grand and
historic. Access to most of them is difficult, but it is worth
applying to the City of London Information Centre early in
each year for part of the small allocation of tickets which they
receive every February. The companies participating in the
scheme vary, but have recently included the Goldsmiths, the
Tallow Chandlers, the Skinners, the Fishmongers, the
Ironmongers and the Haberdashers. Groups of up to 30 can
arrange an appointment to be shown around the magnificent
Fishmongers' Hall at other times by contacting the archivist –
0171-626 3531 ext 257. (Note that the hall is closed
end July-end Sep.)*

London Silver Vaults WC2
Chancery House, Chancery Lane
0171-242 3844   2–2D
*This intriguing, subterranean shopping mall, with its 38 silver
dealers, claims to offer the largest collection of silverware
under one roof in the world. All the items are for sale, with
prices ranging from £5 to £500,000, but you're quite
welcome just to go and browse. / Times: Mon-Fri 09.00-17.30,
Sat 09.00-13.00; Tube: Chancery Lane.*

Lothbury Gallery EC2
41 Lothbury   0171-726 1642   5–2C
*This gallery opened in 1997 and is in the imposing '20s
marble interior of the NatWest HQ in the City. The
permanent exhibition* Time Present and Time Past *traces
developments in banking from the introduction of paper
money to electronic payments, and items on view include the
oldest surviving English cheque. There is also a series of
changing displays of works from the Group's art collection
which includes items from c17 to the present day, with a
focus on c20 British art. / Times: Mon-Fri (not Bank Hols)
10.00-16.00; Tube: Bank.*

Marx Memorial Library * EC1
37A Clerkenwell Green   0171-253 1485   5–1A
*The library is a resource centre for the Labour movement
(and reference to it – as opposed to a tour of the building –
carries a small membership charge). It was set up in 1933
to commemorate the 50th anniversary of the death of Marx,
in an historic Clerkenwell building that dates from 1737.
On special days, for example, Open House (see also) you
may be able to see the basement tunnels which predate the
house and whose origin and purpose remain a mystery.
/ Times: individuals and groups are welcome but the latter need to make an
appointment and are subject to a charge; building Mon 13.00-18.00, Tue, Wed
& Thu 13.00-20.00, Sat 10.00-13.00; closed Aug; Tube: Farringdon.*

Museum and Library of the Order of St John EC1

St John's Gate, St John's Ln   0171-253 6644   5–1A

The ground floor of St John's Gate houses the historic collections of the Order which include Maltese silver and furniture, arms and armour. All items reflect the history and work of the Knights Hospitaller from the time of the Crusades to the present day. Tours can be arranged of the Museum and also the rest of St John's Gate (see also). The reference library is open by appointment. / Times: Mon-Fri 09.00-17.00, Sat 10.00-16.00; Tube: Farringdon.

Museum of London * EC2

London Wall   0171-600 3699   5–2B

One of London's most interesting and best presented museums offers permanent and temporary exhibitions revealing the history of the capital from prehistoric times to the present day. Changing displays might cover anything from photographs of football fans to panels and displays about royal fashion. Star exhibits include the spectacular gilded Lord Mayor's coach (wheeled out once a year for the eponymous Show – see also) to a genuine c18 prison cell complete with prisoners' graffiti. At lunchtimes there are also occasional free lectures and films. / Times: Tue-Sun 16.30-18.00, incl Bank Hol Mons; Tube: Barbican, Bank, St Paul's, Moorgate; Café.

Museum of St Bartholomew's Hospital EC1

West Smithfield   0171-601 8152   5–2B

Original archives, artefacts and medical instruments, together with video and sound recordings, tell the story of this famous hospital from its foundation in 1123 to the present day. Of particular interest is Henry VIII's Charter preventing the closure of the hospital during the Dissolution of the Monasteries. / Times: Tue-Fri 10.00-16.00; Tube: Barbican, St Paul's.

Museum of the Hon Artillery Company EC1

Armoury House, City Rd   0171-382 1537   5–1C

The Honorable Artillery Company was founded in 1537 by Henry VIII from the existing Guild of St George. It was directed to "attend to the Better Defence of the Realm" and encouraged to exercise in handling bows and handguns. The Museum was set up in 1987 to commemorate the Company's 450th anniversary. Highlights include uniforms, Chinese porcelain with the HAC coat of arms, and swords. Donations appreciated. / Times: visits & tours by (telephone) appointment; Tube: Moorgate, Liverpool Street (or tube to Old Street).

National Museum of Cartoon Art * EC1

0171-405 4717

The Trust organises exhibitions of all forms of cartoon art, many free. It does not currently have a permanent display space but takes over venues around town. For details of what exhibition is showing where and when, call the number given, or send an SAE for a free newsletter to New House, 67-68 Hatton Garden, London EC1N 8JY.

National Postal Museum EC1
King Edward St   0171-600 8914   5–2B
This huge philatelic collection is, post-1900, almost completely comprehensive, world-wide. The star attraction is the only complete sheet of Penny Blacks – in fact, it is the proof sheet, printed before the main run. After a visit here why not nip across the road with your sandwiches to Postman's Park (see also). / Times: Mon-Fri 09.30-16.30; Tube: St Paul's.

Nelson Collection EC3
Lloyd's of London, 1 Lime St   0171-327 6260   5–3D
The Collection covers the long war with France following the French Revolution, and the naval victories ending with Trafalgar (1805). Exhibits include ceremonial swords, silver, letters and the original logbook kept by the Master of a warship involved in the Battle of Trafalgar. / Times: by appointment, at least seven days (written) notice required to Curator; Tube: Monument.

Old Bailey EC4
Newgate St   0171-248 3277   5–2B
The Central Criminal Court, as it is more properly called, is the site of London's most notorious trials. All human life is there, and there's usually something intriguing, amusing or just plain bizarre to listen to. There are two public gallery entrances: Warwick Passage, off Old Bailey, and Newgate Street. / Times: Mon-Fri 10.30-13.00, 14.00-16.00; Tube: St Paul's.

Prince Henry's Room EC4
17 Fleet St   0171-936 2710   5–2A
One of the few City buildings to survive the Great Fire, this small room (which has no real royal associations) retains its original panelling and plaster work. It now houses a selection of Samuel Pepys memorabilia. The curators, who are enthusiasts for the great diarist, are pleased to share their knowledge with visitors. / Times: 11.00-14.00; closed Sun, Bank Hols and Sats before Banks Hols; Tube: Temple.

Museums of the Royal College of Surgeons WC2
35-43 Lincoln's Inn Fields   0171-973 2190   5–2A
The College has four collections: the Hunterian Museum, Odontological Museum, and the Wellcome Museums of Pathology and Anatomy. Highlights include: John Hunter's c18 specimen collection; c19 preparations of skulls and teeth by Sir John Tomes, father of British dentistry; and displays of dental pathology in animals. The Hunterian Museum also has paintings by George Stubbs; the 7' 10" skeleton of Charles O'Brien, the Irish giant and c18 surgical instruments. Donations encouraged. Children under 14 must be accompanied. Check with the Visitors Co-ordinator before setting out. / Times: Hunterian and Odontological Museums Mon-Fri 10.00-17.00; Wellcome Museums Mon-Fri 09.00-17.00 by appointment; Tube: Holborn, Temple.

Royal Mail Mount Pleasant Sorting Office EC1

Farringdon Rd   0171-239 2191   5–1A

*If you've always wondered how the mail gets distributed, a
visit here should answer your questions. There are tours at
14.00 or 14.30 on Mon and Wed. They cover the sorting
office, the mechanical sorting equipment and the Mail Rail –
the unstaffed underground railway which distributes post
around the capital. To arrange a visit, call to book in –
individuals are welcome. You will have to confirm in writing
by two weeks before you go. Children under nine are not
admitted. / Tube: Farringdon, King's Cross, Chancery Lane.*

St John Ambulance Exhibition EC1

Priory House, St John's Ln   0171-253 6644   5–1A

*Opposite St John's Gate (see also), this new museum is
to house items from the formation of the St John Ambulance
Association in 1887. The exhibition include training
equipment, photographs and displays illustrating the activities
of the Association in times of war. / Times: call; Tube: Farringdon.*

Saint John's Gate EC1

St John's Lane, Clerkenwell   0171-253 6644   5–1A

*Built in 1504, the Gate was the entrance to the English HQ
of the crusading Knights Hospitallers and has been variously
a coffee house and a tavern. It is now the base of the British
Order of St John, and home to the Museum and Library of
the Order of St John (see also). Tours take in parts of the
building (including the museum) not usually open to the
public. These areas include the Crypt (one of London's few
remaining Norman buildings) and the Cloister Gardens.
Donations are appreciated. / Times: Mon-Fri 10.00-17.00, Sat
10.00-16.00; tours Tue, Fri & Sat 11.00 & 14.30; Tube: Farringdon, Barbican.*

Wesley's Chapel EC1

49 City Rd   0171-253 2262   5–1C

*John Wesley, the father of Methodism, had his Chapel and
house built in 1778 to the designs of George Dance the
Younger. You can visit the chapel (containing his brother
Charles's organ), and Wesley's tomb, which are part of this
fine group of Georgian buildings on the northern fringe of
the City. (Wesley's House and the Museum of Methodism
can also be visited, but for these there is a charge.)
/ Times: Mon-Sat 10.00-16.00 (Sun 12.30); closed Thu 12.45-13.15;
Tube: Old Street, Moorgate*

Outdoor attractions

Broadgate * EC2
0171-505 4000   5–2D
*One summer (end May-beginning of Sep) lunchtime, when
the weather is hot, why not visit the City's Broadgate
development. Most weekdays between 12.30 and 14.00, this
Manhattan-style complex of offices, shops and restaurants
puts on musical or other entertainments (usually at some
point including a display of Spanish dressage with Andalucian
horses). Giant chess and draughts sets are provided, too. A
monthly diary of events – Broadgate Live – is available from
the Arena office (or you can call to be put on the mailing list).*
/ *Tube: Liverpool Street.*

Inns of Court
5–2A
*Lawyers have clustered around the City since the earliest
times. Even today, every barrister practising in England and
Wales must be a member of one of the four inns of court
(the Middle and Inner Temples, Gray's and Lincoln's Inns).*

*All of the inns give the public access to some part of their
territories, which are peaceful, charming and often of
considerable antiquity.*

*Starting in the Temple, don't miss Middle Temple Hall,
a large Tudor hall with a magnificent double hammer-beam
roof. This area is also rich in historical trivia: not only was
Twelfth Night first performed in the hall here by the Bard's
own company, but the Wars of the Roses took their name
from red and white blooms plucked from the garden behind.
The hall at the neighbouring Inner Temple is not open to the
public, but the main sight there is the Temple Church, the
only circular church in London and one of London's oldest
buildings (c12). Leaving the Temple, and progressing up
Chancery Lane, you come first to Lincoln's Inn, with its fine,
sweeping lawns, halls (one c15, one c19) and library, and
then to Gray's Inn, whose chapel and walks are open to public
view. Organised groups can see the inside of the rest of the
building, including the medieval hall, by writing to the Under
Treasurer, Honorable Society of Gray's Inn, Treasury Office,
8 South Square, London WC1R 5EU.*

*The grounds of all the inns are open on weekdays.
Mid-morning and mid-afternoons of weekdays are generally
the best times to gain access to the halls and chapels – if you
are making a special trip it may be wise to confirm access
with the following numbers for the respective inns (all 0171-):
Middle Temple (427 4800), 10.00-11.30, 14.00-16.00, free
tours by appointment, individuals welcome; Lincoln's Inn
(405 1393) 07.00-19.00; and Gray's Inn (405 8164).*
/ *Tube: Temple, Chancery Lane.*

The Monument * EC2
5–3C
The Great Fire of 1666 swept away much of the medieval
City. The burghers of the day commissioned Wren to
memorialise this devastation and the Monument – still the
highest free-standing stone column in the world – was the
result. Its height (202 feet) is the same as its distance from
the baker's shop in Pudding Lane where the fire started.
The story is given in detail in the large notice at the base of
the column. You can climb to the top but there's a small
charge. / Tube: Monument.

Riverside walk
See the South section for suggestions of interesting walks by
the Thames.

Tower Bridge * SE1
0171-407 0922
Bridge Lift Information Line: 0171-378 7700   5–4D
One of London's great symbols, the bridge was built between
1886 and 1894. Despite its appearance, it is, in fact, a
thoroughly modern steel structure, but was clad in stone to
harmonise with the Tower of London. The halves of the bridge
(which was originally steam-powered, but is now electrically
operated) can still be raised to accommodate large vessels
needing access to the Pool of London – ring the number given
to find out when the bridge is next scheduled to be raised.
There is a fascinating display inside the bridge, but at quite a
significant charge. / Tube: Tower Hill.

Tower of London * EC3
West Gate, Tower of London   0171-709 0765   5–3D
The Tower of London is one of the most interesting and
historic sites in London and unfortunately charges handsomely
for entering its precincts or visiting the treasures within
(which, of course, include the Crown Jewels). You can get a
good perspective of the medieval building from the riverside
walk, however (and see also Ceremony of the Keys).
/ Tube: Tower Hill.

The East End

Introduction

Centuries of being the poor relation among the areas of London, has left the East End with a very different range of amenities from any other area. It means for example that in the inner city there is only one park of any note, **Victoria Park**. However, if you are prepared to go as far as the end of the Central Line, you will, in **Epping Forest**, find the largest medieval woodland anywhere near London. A feature of the East End (and much less common elsewhere), which is of particular interest to children, is the city farms.

As regeneration of the East End proper takes hold, however, some very notable attractions are springing up. **Canary Wharf**, the largest office development in Europe, has given the Isle of Dogs the second tallest building in Europe. The redevelopment of **St Katharine's Dock** has created what is by far the nicest marina in inner London, and, on a sunny day, a really charming place. The continuing efforts to improve the **Lee Valley** are beginning to make it an amenity which offers a large range of attractions.

The area is well served with non-commercial art galleries (the **Whitechapel Gallery** being the grandest and longest established).

For people-watching and browsing, the area has several of the most characterful markets in London: **Petticoat** and **Brick Lanes**, and **Columbia Road Flower Market**. They are particularly popular Sunday morning destinations.

London Docklands Visitor Centre E14
3 Limeharbour, Isle of Dogs   0171-512 1111   1–3D
This is not just an information centre on what to do in Docklands and East London. There's also an exhibition and an audio-visual presentation on the changing face of the area. With around 50 leaflets on what to see and do in the area, this is a good place to pick up information, including illustrated brochures detailing local walks. The Street Guide *includes a usefully indexed map. / Times: Mon-Fri 08.30-18.00; Sat, Sun and Bank Hols 09.30-17.00; Tube: Crossharbour (DLR).*

Redbridge Tourist Information Centre, Essex
The Town Hall, 128-142 High Rd, Ilford
0181-478 3020   off map
/ Times: Mon-Fri 08.30-17.00; Rail: Ilford.

Tower Hamlets Tourist Information Centre E1
107A Commercial St   0171-375 2549   5–2D
/ Times: Mon-Fri 09.30-13.30 & 14.00-16.30; Tube: Liverpool Street.

Indoor attractions

Bethnal Green Museum of Childhood E2
Cambridge Heath Rd   0181-983 5200   1–2D
Housing the V&A's collection of toys, games, puppets, dolls and dolls houses (of which there are over 40), this repository of children's memorabilia offers quite enough to interest children and parents. There are workshops for children on most Saturdays, and school holiday activities. The museum has an excellent supply of free literature about London attractions, particularly those in the East End. / Times: Mon-Sat 10.00-17.50, Sun 14.30-17.50; Tube: Bethnal Green; Café.

Brooking Collection, Kent
University of Greenwich, Dartford Campus, Oakfield Lane, Dartford   0181-331 9897   off map
Windows rescued from Windsor, doorknobs from 10 Downing Street ... this unique and comprehensive collection of architectural details from the past five centuries includes doors, staircase sections, boot-scrapers and rainwater heads. Many visit because they have a period house which they want to restore or refurbish and want a point of reference. Information on more than 7,000 items is held on computer and examples of details of specific types or particular periods can be retrieved prior to the visit. / Times: by appointment, 09.00-17.00 (also weekends and evenings for groups); Rail: Dartford (then 476 bus).

Camerawork E2
121 Roman Rd   0181-980 6256   1–2D
Exhibitions at this contemporary photographic gallery are usually thematic (frequently based on social issues) and often include less conventional media such as computer output and video. / Times: Tue-Sat 13.00-18.00; Tube: Bethnal Green.

Chisenhale Gallery E3
64 Chisenhale Rd   0181-981 4518   1–2D
This contemporary gallery holds half a dozen mixed media shows a year by British and foreign artists. / Times: Wed-Sun 13.00-18.00; Tube: Mile End, Bethnal Green.

Clowns Gallery E8
1 Hillman St   0171-608 0312   1–1D
As the name suggests, you will find all sorts of artefacts and archive material relating to clowns at this museum/gallery opposite Hackney Town Hall. Parents beware! There is also a joke shop kids will want to spend their pocket money in. The evening of the first Friday in the month is a 'social' with speakers and films, for example, on subjects of clownish interest – donations welcome. / Times: 1st Fri of month 11.00-16.00, also 19.00 (for 20.00 start); other times by arrangement including groups of up to 50; Rail: Hackney Central.

Forest & Co E15
17-31 Gibbins Rd   0181-534 2931   1–2D
*Sales include everything from cars through carpets, jewellery,
bric-à-brac and antiques. Go to this official auctioneers for
Customs and Excise (also private vendors and bailiffs) to
listen to the patter.* / Times: alternate Thu from 11.00; Tube: Stratford.

Geffrye Museum E2
Kingsland Rd   0171-739 9893   1–2D
*This is a rather special museum, in elegant early c18
almshouses, which tells the story of English domestic interiors
through a series of period rooms, from Elizabethan times to
the 1950s. There's also an enchanting walled herb garden.
In summer the museum organises unusual, intelligent
activities for kids and there is often music (not always period),
inside or in the garden – ask for a programme. Most
Londoners will never have been here – they should go.*
/ Times: Tue-Sat 10.00-17.00, Sun and Bank Hols 14.00-17.00;
Tube: Liverpool Street, Old Street; Café.

Hackney Museum E8
Central Hall, Mare St   0181-986 6914   1–1D
*The museum celebrates the history of Hackney from Viking
times in a programme of changing exhibitions, but it's the
displays that reflect the area's cultural diversity which are the
particular attraction. Perhaps of special interest to local
residents is Hackney Voices a CD-ROM of information,
photographs and interviews with first-generation Hackney
residents about their experiences of settling in the borough.
For children the Holiday Club consists of two workshops a
week during school holidays.* / Times: Tue-Fri 10.00-17.00,
Sat 13.30-17.00; Rail: Hackney Central.

Hilliard & Sparey E1
26 Spital Square, Spitalfields   0171-375 1176   5–1D
*Watch the metalwork artists cut and weld (that is to say,
create a lot of sparks and flames). They made all the gates
around the market, and you might see them forming
balustrades, or creating chairs or garden furniture, for
example.* / Times: Mon-Fri 10.00-18.00; Tube: Liverpool Street.

London Chest Hospital E2
Third Floor, Bonner Rd, Victoria Park
0171-377 7608   1–2D
*The Capel Collection consists of 25 instruments and books
of/on instruments relating to chest medicine collected since
the Hospital was founded in 1848. The Trust has a larger,
more general collection at the Royal London Hospital
(see also).* / Times: by (written) appointment; Tube: Bethnal Green.

London Gas Museum E3

Twelvetrees Crescent   0171-538 4982   1–2D

A small museum, illustrating the history of the gas industry (and what life was like before gas). There is an exhibit commemorating the Beckton Gasworks (in nearby E16) which were, in their time, the largest in the world. / Times: 09.00-16.00 (by appointment, individuals welcome); Tube: Bromley-by-Bow.

Manor Park Museum E12

Romford Rd, Manor Park   0181-514 0274   off map

The museum has been moved around the borough over the past years and is now in the old reading room of the library. It offers local history displays (geared towards schools' requirements), and there is a room for temporary exhibitions. / Times: Tue, Fri & Sat 10.00-17.00, Thu 13.00-20.00; Rail: Manor Park.

Matt's Gallery E3

42-44 Copperfield Rd   0181-983 1771   1–2D

This contemporary gallery commissions works, ranging from installations which are made in, and specifically for, the space, to video, photography and painting exhibitions. / Times: Wed-Sun 12.00-18.00 (exhibitions); Tube: Mile End.

North Woolwich Old Station Museum E16

Pier Rd, North Woolwich   0171-474 7244   off map

This restored Victorian station, now a museum, tells the story of the local railways of east London and their impact on the areas they served. There are tickets, timetables, posters, a reconstructed '20s ticket office and, of course, trains. The first Sunday of every month (Easter-Oct) is a steam day. Occasionally, there are film shows and model railway days. There are kids events during school holidays – book places in advance. / Times: Fri & Sun 14.00-17.00; Sat 10.00-17.00; Summer hols Mon-Wed 14.00-17.00, free activities for kids 14.00-16.00; Sat 10.00-17.00, Sun & Bank Hols 14.00-17.00; Tube: East Ham (then 101 bus), Stratford (then 69 bus), North Woolwich.

Plashet Zoo E7

Plashet Park, Shrewsbury Rd, Forest Gate
0181-503 5994   off map

If you would like to see animals more exotic than you will find in a city farm, why not visit the collection here – year round, you can laugh at the llamas, wave at the wallabies, ogle the owls and gawp at the goats. There are also falconry displays, and in summer (May-Sep) you can see tropical butterflies emerging, flying and feeding. Other reasons to visit include the Pheasant Phenomenon aviaries. / Times: summer Tue-Sun 10.00-17.00; winter Tue-Sun 10-16.00; Tube: East Ham (or rail to Woodgrange Park); Café.

Ragged School Museum E3

46-50 Copperfield Rd   0181-980 6405   1–2D

This museum of the history of the East End is housed in a Victorian canalside warehouse which, from 1895, formed part of the largest ragged (free) school in London. Appropriately, education and the life and work of Dr Barnardo are given particular emphasis, and there is a recreated Victorian classroom (which is used by school groups for re-enacted Victorian lessons). During the school holidays, activities are organised, from making Victorian sweets to treasure hunts. All are popular and space is limited – call for a free programme. / Times: Wed & Thu 10.00-17.00, 1st Sun of month 14.00-17.00; Tube: Mile End; Café.

Royal London Hospital Archives E1

St Augustine with St Philip's Church, Newark St
0171-377 7608   1–2D

The permanent exhibition about the history of the famous hospital is housed in the basement of a c19 church. Highlights include: a small Hogarth drawing; a copy of George Washington's false teeth (the originals are on loan to a museum in America); documents relating to Elephant Man Joseph Merrick (and a copy of his hat); and a bust of, and watercolours by, WWI heroine Edith Cavell (who trained here). There are also videos, including films from the 1930s showing what it was like being a nurse then, and what it is like today. / Times: Mon-Fri 10.00-16.30 (occasionally closed 13.00-14.00); Tube: Whitechapel.

The Showroom E2

44 Bonner Rd   0181-983 4115   1–2D

As at the other two galleries nearby (Matt's and the Chisenhale), the contemporary works displayed here are often installation-based, but may include performance art and videos. / Times: Wed-Sun 13.00-18.00 (exhibitions); Tube: Bethnal Green.

Spitalfields Market E1

Brushfield St   0171-247 6590   5–2D

The City's former fruit and vegetable market (vacated in 1991) is now run by the same company as Camden Lock. It has been transformed into a mixed development that is particularly popular on Sundays. The centrepiece is a fantastical sculpture around which are stalls selling arts and crafts, bric-à-brac and organic food. There is an international food hall as well as sports facilities and an opera house. Regular special events include an Alternative Fashion Week. / Times: Mon-Fri 09.00-18.00, Sun 09.00-15.00; Tube: Liverpool Street.

Thames Museum E1
Thames Divisional HQ, 98 Wapping High St   1–3D
*This collection documents the history of the Marine Police;
artefacts date from 1798 – the date of the first organised
London police force. Weapons, including cutlasses, model
boats and uniforms, are all displayed in a pleasant setting
overlooking the Thames.* / Times: by (written) appointment, groups
and clubs preferred; Tube: Wapping.

Upminster Tithe Barn, Agricultural and Folk Museum, Essex
Hall Lane, Upminster   01708-457266   off map
*The barn is a large thatched, timber-framed structure,
probably built around 1450. It contains a collection illustrating
the farming, urban and social history of the community and
shows the transition of the area from countryside to suburbia.
There are old agricultural implements, farriers' tools, dairying
equipment, bicycles, photographs, laundry paraphernalia
(from the time when it was all done manually), and toys and
games.* / Times: 1st full weekend of each month Apr-Oct inclusive,
14.00-18.00; Rail: Upminster, then 248 bus.

Upminster Windmill, Essex
St Mary's Lane, Upminster   01708-457266   off map
*This white five-storey smock mill was built in the early c19
and worked commercially until around 1935. It is owned by
the London Borough of Havering and staffed by members of
Hornchurch and District Historical Society. The mill has
undergone substantial repair and is hoped to be working
again by 2001.* / Times: Apr-Sep, 3rd Sat & Sun of month, 14.00-17.30
and National Mills Day (2nd Sun in May); Rail: Upminster Bridge (or tube to
Upminster).

Valence House Museum, Essex
Becontree Avenue, Dagenham   0181-595 8404   off map
*This partly moated, mainly c17 manor house contains various
artefacts, from the Stone Age onwards, which have been
found locally. Its most notable contents, perhaps, are fine
portraits of the Fanshawe family, including some by Lely and
Kneller. There are also domestic interiors from the c17 and
c20, displays on the history of Dagenham Village, and a
walled herb garden. Children's workshops are held
periodically.* / Times: Tue-Fri 09.30-13.00 & 14.00-16.30, Sat 10.00-16.00;
Rail: Chadwell Heath; Café Sat only.

Vestry House Museum E17
Vestry Rd, Walthamstow   0181-509 1917   off map
This prettily situated workhouse (1730) was converted into a museum of local history in the 1930s. It is in the old village of Walthamstow (which is worth a visit in its own right). The most singular exhibit is probably the Bremer Car, which is claimed to be one of the first petrol-driven cars to be made in London. An original police cell (used between 1840 and 1870) is another curiosity. There is a programme of temporary exhibitions. / Times: Mon-Fri 10.00-13.00, 14.00-17.30 (Sat 17.00), closed Bank Hols; Tube: Walthamstow Central.

West Ham United E13
Green St, Upton Park   0181-548 2748   1–2D
The Hammers is the only London club that opens up for regular free open days. If you would like to go backstage at the Boleyn Ground, then telephone to book yourself onto one of the tours that take place on the first Thursday of each month at 10.00 during the season. Individuals are welcome. / Tube: Upton Park.

Whitechapel Art Gallery E1
80 Whitechapel High St   0171-522 7888   5–2D
This important non-commercial venue, in its atmospheric, purpose-built Edwardian building, has no permanent collection. It can therefore make a virtue of necessity, presenting an ever-changing series of exhibitions of c20 and contemporary art, often of challenging artists. For details call the recorded information line (tel 0171-522 7878). There is a programme of talks around the exhibitions, and sometimes also early-evening films. / Times: Tue-Sun 11.00-17.00, Wed 11.00-20.00; Tube: Aldgate East; Café.

Whitechapel Bell Foundry * E2
32-34 Whitechapel Rd   0171-247 2599   1–2D
The foundry – where America's Liberty Bell was cast – is sited in a coaching inn dating from 1638. There is a charge for tours of the foundry itself (one of only two in the UK and the only one that still does everything by hand), but there is a small free museum. Over the entrance door is 'Big Ben' – a full-size wooden template of the famous Westminster bell, cast at the foundry in 1858. It is worth paying a visit to the loo – the trip takes you through the small yard with a c12 Burmese bell, with dragon centrepiece. / Times: Mon-Fri 09.00-17.00; Tube: Aldgate East.

Whitewebbs Museum of Transport, Middx
Whitewebbs Rd, Enfield   0181-367 1898   off map

If you are interested in vintage vehicles, head for this former pumping station, where the collection on display includes motorbikes, cars, bicycles and a 1912 fire engine. The late c19 building – now painstaking restored by enthusiasts – was operative for only 30 years, until the river was straightened and bypassed the station! The museum remains surprisingly little known. / Times: Mon-Fri 10.00-17.00 (but call first); Rail: Crews Hill.

William Morris Gallery E17
Lloyd Park, Forest Rd   0181-527 3782   off map

William Morris, born in Walthamstow in 1834, was probably the most influential designer and craftsman London has ever produced. He died in 1896, but his ideas were carried on by the Arts and Crafts movement into the 1920s, and many of his designs, especially for wallpaper, are still in production today. This delightful c18 house in its own grounds contains a display of Morris's work and personal memorabilia, together with examples of the products of his associates, Burne-Jones, Rossetti and Philip Webb. (For further information you can visit http://www.lbwf.gov.uk/wmg.) / Times: Tue-Sat & 1st Sun of month 10.00-13.00 & 14.00-17.00; Tube: Walthamstow Central.

Outdoor attractions

Brick Lane E1, E2
1–2D

Forget the 'papers – roll up at 6 o'clock in the morning, or a little after if you must, to start off Sunday with a truly East End 'pile it high, sell it cheap' experience. 'It' might be almost anything. / Times: Sun 06.00-13.00; Tube: Aldgate, Aldgate East, Liverpool Street, Shoreditch (closed at time of going to press).

Canary Wharf E14
0171-418 2783 (box office/events information)   1–3D

Cesar Pelli's great tower (244m high) on the Isle of Dogs is, at 50 storeys, the tallest building in Britain. You don't need to approach it to appreciate it – you can see it from all over London – but if you do, there's an impressive shopping mall at its base with more than 60 shops and restaurants. There are other shiny, new buildings around the tower's base, which are worth a view, as well as public spaces. In Cabot Square, look for the unusual fountain which is controlled, via computer, by the speed and direction of the wind. There is a regular programme of arts and events, many of which are free, including outside events in the summer. / Tube: Canary Wharf (DLR).

The East End

Columbia Road Flower Market E2
Columbia Rd   5–1D
Every Sunday morning this east London street (with a few neighbouring alleys) bursts into bloom – you'll know you are near the market when you see the occasional palm tree walking through the streets, possibly in the company of perambulating shrubs and boxes of herbs. It's best to arrive early – it gets terribly crowded. A trip here combines well with a visit to Spitalfields Market and Brick Lane. / Times: Sun 08.00-12.30; Tube: Old Street, Liverpool Street (Shoreditch was closed at the time of going to press).

East Ham Nature Reserve E6
Norman Rd, East Ham   0181-470 4525   off map
The two suburban nature trails here have the mission of introducing everyone to the joys of nature. Set in London's largest churchyard (in use since Norman times, though the oldest stones date from c17), the trails are fully accessible (including to people in wheelchairs). A highly informative, illustrated guide, is available from the Visitor Centre – a Braille version is also available. Ring to ensure the reserve is open before you set off. / Times: Tue-Fri 10.00-17.00, Sat & Sun 13.00-16.00; Tube: East Ham.

Epping Forest, Essex
0181-508 0028   off map
Two miles by 12, this ancient forest on the eastern fringe of London (owned by the Corporation of London since Victorian times) is the largest open space in Essex. Much effort is put into maintaining the landscape, with its diverse natural history, and much of the area is designated as a Site of Special Scientific Interest. Although the forest is a very popular destination, it's big enough that you can loose yourself in it – real countryside AND accessible from a tube station!
A particular attraction is Queen Elizabeth's Hunting Lodge (small charge to visit), near Chingford, which is the only surviving Tudor 'hunt-standing' (from which the monarch could view the hunt's progress). The Information Centre at High Beech organises occasional walks year-round through the forest (details from the number given). At this spot (it's around two miles from Loughton), there is an easy-access path and also tracks that are popular with riders of horses and mountain bikes. / Times: information centre, summer, 10.00 (Sun 11.00)-17.00; winter, call for hours; Tube: Epping, Theydon Bois, Loughton, Snaresbrook.

The Greenway
0181-472 1430 (Planning or Leisure Services)
Formerly less romantically described as the Northern Outfall Sewer Embankment, this elevated feature of the landscape was built in the 1860s to provide a sewage and drainage system for East London. Its path is about four miles long, with pedestrian and cycle access points, which runs from High Street South in E6, to Wick Lane in E3 (with a short section just north of the A11 that is closed off). The route is being extended as far as Royal Docks Road, in the Docklands. At its western end it provides tantalising glimpses of Abbey Mills Pumping Station, the flamboyant Victorian 'Cathedral of Sewage'. The way is being developed as a wildlife habitat, and noticeboards tell you about flora and fauna. / Tube: east end Beckton (DLR) (or west end, rail to Homerton).

Greenwich Foot Tunnel E14
0181-854 8888 ext 5493 (to confirm lift times)   1–3D
The tunnel, opened in 1902, connects Greenwich with the Isle of Dogs and was built because the steamboat ferry was contributing to excessive congestion of the river at this point. It lies ten metres below the low water mark, is 390 metres long and made of cast iron segments, lined with concrete and tiled. New lifts were installed in 1992, replacing equipment which had lasted since 1904; the original wood panelling was retained, however. Although the tunnel has a mainly practical function, children of all ages may feel walking under the Thames is an end in itself. / Times: lift service, Mon-Sat 07.00-19.00, Sun 10.00-17.30; tunnel 24 hours; Rail: Greenwich, Island Gardens (DLR).

Hackney City Farm E2
1a Goldsmith's Row   0171-729 6381   1–2D
Hackney City Farm keeps as full a range as possible of traditional farm livestock in its 1 1/2-acre site. It also boasts bees, and is proud of its prize-winning herd of pedigree saddleback pigs. In spring, the lambs and calves are a particular reason to take the children. / Times: Tue-Sun 10.00-16.30 (and Bank Hols); Tube: Bethnal Green; Café.

Hainault Forest Country Park, Essex
0181-500 7353   off map
This square mile of woodland was dedicated to the public in 1906 and is one of the few remaining vestiges of the great forest of Essex and Waltham (see also Epping Forest). It is a Site of Special Scientific Interest because of the ancient woodland, pollarded trees and flora and fauna. Foxburrows Farm conserves rare breeds and employs traditional farm practices, such as haymaking. There is also an orienteering course. Activities in the summer events programme might include a storytelling picnic, a fungi-finding expedition and a bat search. / Times: 07.00-dusk; Tube: Hainault then 247 or 362 bus (or rail to Romford or Ilford then 150 or 247 bus); Café.

The East End

Hainault Lodge Nature Reserve, Essex
0181-500 7353 (Hainault Country Park)   off map
*Redbridge Borough's first Local Nature Reserve is remarkable
for its views across London and the variety of habitats within
its small area. You need to obtain permission (from Hainault
Country Park, see previous entry) to enter the 14-acre site,
(adjacent to the Park), but everyone is welcome and tours can
be arranged. Creatures you might see include many nesting
birds and small mammals – if you are very lucky you might
spot the rare Black Rabbit.* / Tube: Hainault then 247 or 362 bus (or
rail to Romford or Ilford then 150 or 247 bus).

Island History Trust E14
Island House, Roserton St   0171-987 6041   1–3D
*Documenting the social history of the Isle of Dogs, the 5,000
pictures – from the 1870s to the 1960s – in this collection
show street scenes, churches, sport, work, social lives, pubs
and churches. All are captioned and indexed and so of
particular interest to people who have a connection with the
area or who wish to research family history.* / Times: by (telephone)
appointment; Rail: Crossharbour (DLR).

Lee Valley
Enquiries to: Countryside Centre, Abbey Gardens,
Waltham Abbey, Essex EN9 1XQ   01992-713838
*Since 1967, the derelict valley of the River Lee has been
being transformed into a 'green chain', extending out from
Hackney, via Tottenham and Enfield, to the more truly rural
delights of Hertfordshire and Essex. You can walk the whole
23 miles on the towpath, or cycle it – it is part of the
National Cycle Network linking Hertfordshire with Harwich.
It's still something of a patchwork at the moment, but there's
already a variety of things to see and do. Natural attractions
include a variety of bird life and a dragonfly sanctuary.
Man-made items of interest include some pretty and historic
c18 buildings, including the most powerful tidal mill ever built
(open Sundays, 14.00-16.00, small charge) and the Clock
Mill. If you're planning a visit, contact the Countryside Centre
which has a small area with displays but is primarily a place
to pick up a variety of relevant leaflets. All parts of the Park
are easily accessible from the rail line which runs alongside.*
/ Times: centre, Mar-Oct, 09.30-17.00 ; Nov-Feb, Tue-Sun 9.30-16.30;
Tube: Tottenham Hale, or rail stations on L'pool St to Cambridge Line.

Mudchute Park and Farm E14
Pier St   0171-515 5901   1–3D
The largest urban farm in London, this 32-acre site is the most significant open space on the Isle of Dogs. It includes a riding arena, fields, a wild section, a picnic area and thousands of trees which have been planted in the past five years. Because it's several times bigger than most of the others, it can be run largely as if it were a small farm in the country – complete with its own grassland for grazing. On the livestock front, the speciality here is sheep, of which a wide variety are kept, but there are also cattle, goats and pigs. Each year there is a family day during July. / Times: 09.00-17.00; Tube: Crossharbour (DLR), Mudchute (DLR); Café.

Newham City Farm E16
King George Avenue   0171-476 1170   off map
This 4 1/2-acre farm has a wide range of livestock, including a shire horse, a donkey, cows, pigs, sheep, goats, chickens, ducks and geese. It is well geared up for casual visitors – 50,000 people pass through the gates each year. Following expansion into the neighbouring King George V Park, there is now a visitor centre. / Times: Tue-Sun 10.00-17.00 (16.00, winter); Tube: Royal Albert (DLR), or tube to Plaistow then 262 bus; in- and outdoor picnic area.

Petticoat Lane E1
Certainly the best-known market in the East End, and possibly in London. The Sunday morning activity here is a phenomenon worth seeing whether or not you have any desire to invest in some of the low-cost clothes which are the market's speciality. / Times: Sun 09.00-14.00; Tube: Liverpool Street, Fenchurch Street.

Postman's Park EC1
Little Britain, King Edward St   5–2B
A tiny entrance opposite the National Postal Museum leads into a small and unprepossessing park with benches and grass. However, follow the path and you see a long wooden porch protecting what looks like the rear wall of a block of flats and a slightly raised patio. Set into the wall are around 50 memorials to "heroic men and women", many of which have a story to tell. / Tube: St Paul's, Barbican.

Riverside Walk
See the South section for suggestions of interesting walks by the Thames.

St Katharine's Dock E1
1–3D

St Katharine's by the Tower (as the area is more properly called) is a fine collection of buildings, principally designed by the great c19 engineer Thomas Telford and restored to make a very attractive marina. It offers by far the nicest place for a riverside stroll in central London – the Tower of London and Tower Bridge providing a dramatic backdrop. In the summer, there is lunchtime music several times a week.
/ Tube: Tower Hill; Café.

Spitalfields Community Farm E1
Weaver St   0171-247 8762   1–2D

Despite its small size (1 1/2 acres), and location (on former wasteground) this popular attraction manages to squeeze in most of the usual farm animals. Look out also for special events at Christmas, Easter and Summer, some of which are free. / Times: Tue-Sun 10.00-17.00 (18.00 summer); Tube: Aldgate East (Shoreditch closed at time of going to press).

Stepney Stepping Stones Farm E1
Stepney Way   0171-790 8204   1–2D

This six-acre farm has all the main types of farm animals – cows, pigs, donkeys, sheep, goats, chickens, ducks and geese, as well as rabbits, guinea pigs, ferrets and chipmunks.
There is also a picnic garden, a small library of books relating to farming and a box of children's books and games.
The venture, which has now been in existence for 18 years, is run entirely by volunteers and trainees, and partly funded by the sale of produce and home cooking. There are also events during summer school holidays, some of which are free.
/ Times: Tue-Sun 09.30-18.00; Tube: Stepney Green, Limehouse; Café.

Tower Hamlets Cemetery Park E3
Southern Grove   0181-980 2373   1–2D

Built as a model necropolis for wealthy Londoners in 1841, this 27-acre site was used for burials until 1966. A period of neglect followed, during which the local flora and fauna established themselves with a vengeance – in 1986 Tower Hamlets decided to make a virtue of necessity and declared the place a nature reserve. Some very fine Victorian tombs remain and there is also a tree trail which takes about 45 minutes to complete. An educational facility, the Soanes Centre, was to open after we went to press.
/ Times: 08.30-dusk; Tube: Mile End.

Victoria Park E3

Old Ford Rd   0181-985 1957/6186   1–2D

In the 1840s, concern grew in east London about the lack of any recreation space for the burgeoning population. Fearing unrest, the government sold York House in Westminster to pay for the establishment of the new Victoria Park (of 220 acres), which is still the only large, formal park in the East End. Its style is very much in keeping with its name – it has lakes and fountains, large areas of bedding plants, children's playground, a bandstand that is the site of live music on Sunday afternoons in July and August, and a herd of fallow deer and pygmy goats. Recent years have seen much refurbishment of the facilities. The oldest model boat club in the world meets here most Sunday mornings during summer. The emergency services use the park for their '999 Spectacular', usually in June. / Times: 07.30-dusk; Tube: Bethnal Green, Mile End.

West Ham Park E7

Upton Lane   0181-472 3584   off map

This 77-acre park in West Ham has been owned and run by the Corporation of London since 1874. The recreational facilities include a large children's playground and a seven-acre formal garden in the south east corner of the park. During the summer there are children's entertainers at the bandstand and Sunday afternoon concerts. / Times: 07.30-30 mins before dusk; Tube: Plaistow.

Woolwich Free Ferry

North Woolwich Pier, Ferry Approach   off map

The ferry – the only free automated way to cross the Thames – began in 1889. Paddlesteamers were, alas, replaced by the current, less romantic, design in 1963. If you are lucky, though, the captain might let you climb the steep steps to his eyrie. / Times: Mon-Fri 06.00-20.30, Sat 06.00-20.00, Sun 11.30-19.30; Rail: north of the Thames, North Woolwich; south of the Thames 180 bus.

Maps

MAP 1 – LONDON OVERVIEW

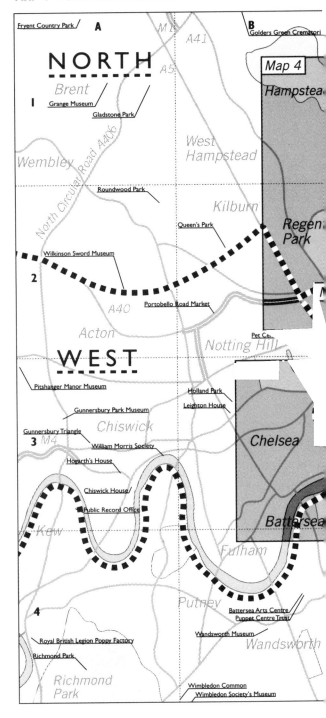

Fryent Country Park

A

B

Golders Green Crematori

NORTH

Map 4

Brent

Hampstea

1

Grange Museum

Gladstone Park

West
Hampstead

Wembley

Roundwood Park

Kilburn

Queen's Park

Regen
Park

2

Wilkinson Sword Museum

A40

Portobello Road Market

Pet Ce...

Acton

Notting Hill

WEST

Pitshanger Manor Museum

Holland Park

Leighton House

Gunnersbury Park Museum

Chiswick

Gunnersbury Triangle

3 *M4*

William Morris Society

Chelsea

Hogarth's House

Chiswick House

Public Record Office

Kew

Battersea

Fulham

Putney

Battersea Arts Centre
Puppet Centre Trust

4

Wandsworth Museum

Wandsworth

Royal British Legion Poppy Factory

Richmond Park

Richmond
Park

Wimbledon Common
Wimbledon Society's Museum

MAP I – LONDON OVERVIEW

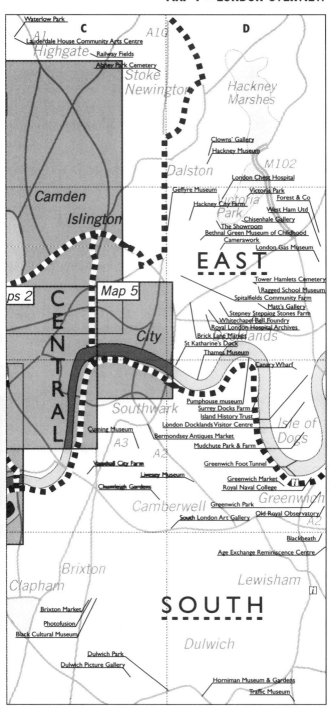

MAP 2 – CENTRAL LONDON

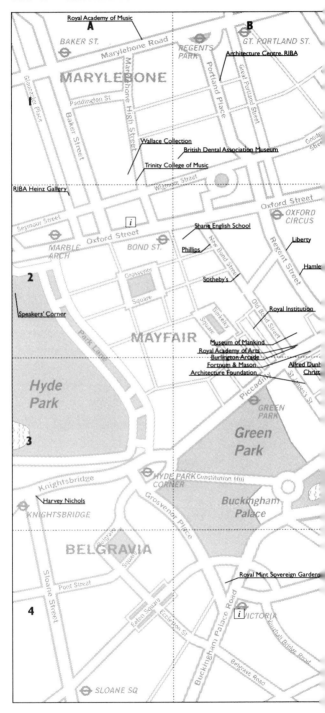

MAP 2 – CENTRAL LONDON

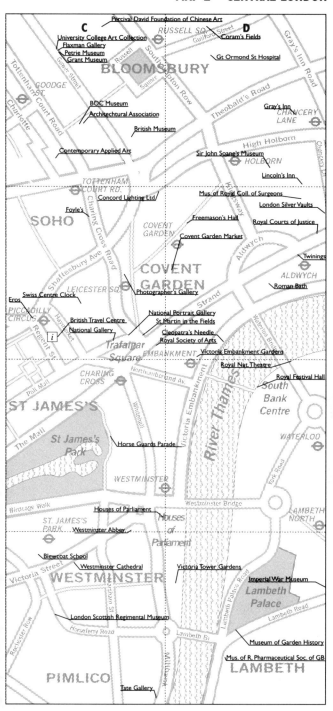

Percival David Foundation of Chinese Art

C · **D**

RUSSELL SQ.

Coram's Fields

University College Art Collection

Flaxman Gallery

Petrie Museum

Grant Museum

Gt Ormond St Hospital

BLOOMSBURY

Theobald's Road

Gray's Inn — **CHANCERY LANE**

BOC Museum

Architectural Association

British Museum

High Holborn

Sir John Soane's Museum — **HOLBORN**

Contemporary Applied Art

Lincoln's Inn

TOTTENHAM COURT RD.

Mus. of Royal Coll. of Surgeons

London Silver Vaults

Concord Lighting Ltd

SOHO

Foyle's

COVENT GARDEN

Freemason's Hall

Royal Courts of Justice

Covent Garden Market

Twinings

COVENT GARDEN

ALDWYCH

Roman Bath

LEICESTER SQ.

Photographer's Gallery

Strand

Swiss Centre Clock

Eros

PICCADILLY CIRCUS

National Portrait Gallery

British Travel Centre

St Martin in the Fields

National Gallery

Cleopatra's Needle

Royal Society of Arts

Trafalgar Square

Victoria Embankment Gardens

EMBANKMENT

Royal Nat. Theatre

CHARING CROSS

Royal Festival Hall

South Bank Centre

ST JAMES'S

WATERLOO

The Mall

St James's Park

Horse Guards Parade

River Thames

WESTMINSTER

Westminster Bridge

LAMBETH NORTH

Birdcage Walk

Houses of Parliament

Houses of Parliament

ST. JAMES'S PARK

Westminster Abbey

Blewcoat School

Westminster Cathedral

Victoria Tower Gardens

Imperial War Museum

WESTMINSTER

Lambeth Palace

London Scottish Regimental Museum

Museum of Garden History

Mus. of R. Pharmaceutical Soc. of GB

PIMLICO

Tate Gallery

LAMBETH

MAP 3 – WEST LONDON (SW POSTCODES)

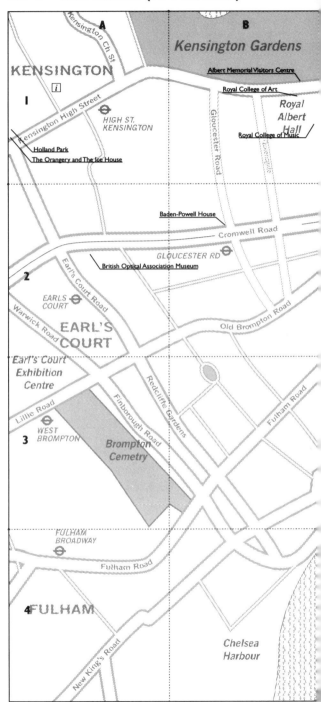

MAP 3 – WEST LONDON (SW POSTCODES)

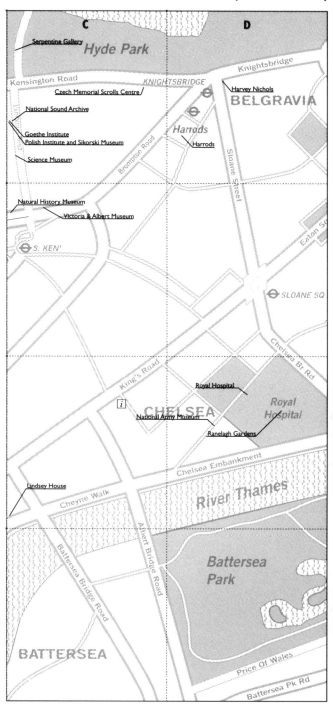

MAP 4 – NORTH LONDON

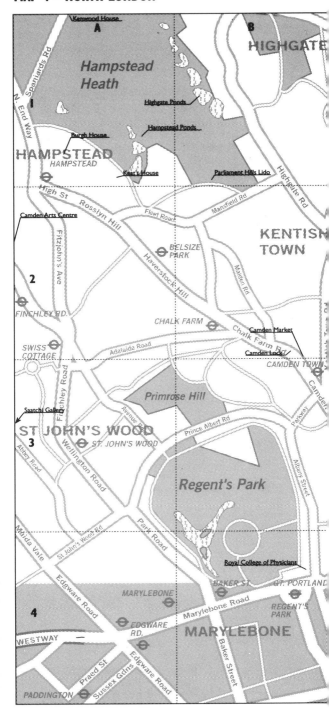

MAP 4 – NORTH LONDON

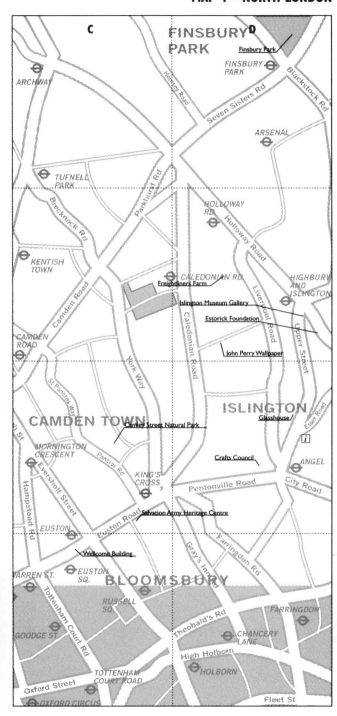

MAP 5 – THE CITY

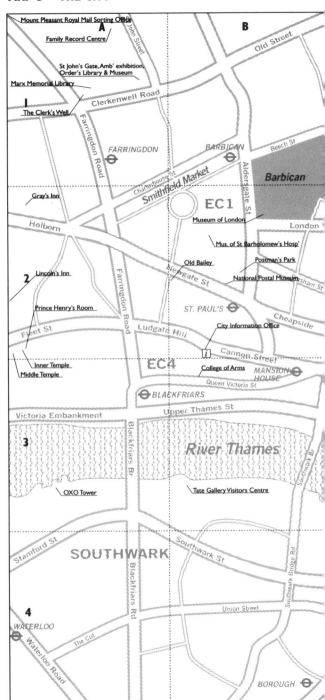

Mount Pleasant Royal Mail Sorting Office — A

B

Old Street

Family Record Centre

St John's Gate, Amb' exhibition,
Order's Library & Museum

Marx Memorial Library

Clerkenwell Road

1

The Clerk's Well

FARRINGDON

BARBICAN

Beech St

Barbican

Gray's Inn

Holborn

Smithfield Market

EC1

Museum of London

London

Mus. of St Bartholomew's Hosp'

Postman's Park

Old Bailey

2 Lincoln's Inn

Newgate St

National Postal Museum

ST. PAUL'S

Cheapside

Prince Henry's Room

Fleet St

Ludgate Hill

City Information Office

Cannon Street

EC4

College of Arms

MANSION HOUSE

Inner Temple

Middle Temple

Queen Victoria St

BLACKFRIARS

Victoria Embankment

Upper Thames St

3

River Thames

Blackfriars Br

Southwark Br

OXO Tower

Tate Gallery Visitors Centre

Stamford St

SOUTHWARK

Southwark St

Blackfriars Rd

Southwark Bridge Rd

4

WATERLOO

Union Street

Waterloo Road

The Cut

BOROUGH

MAP 5 – THE CITY

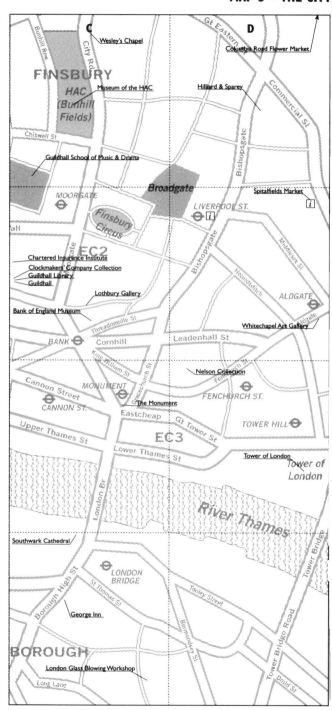

C

Wesley's Chapel

Columbia Road Flower Market

Gt Eastern St

D

Bunhill Row

City Rd

FINSBURY

Commercial St

Museum of the HAC

Hilliard & Sparey

HAC (Bunhill Fields)

Bishopsgate

Chiswell St

Guildhall School of Music & Drama

Broadgate

Spitalfields Market

MOORGATE

LIVERPOOL ST.

Finsbury Circus

EC2

Bishopsgate

Houndsditch

Chartered Insurance Institute
Clockmakers' Company Collection
Guildhall Library
Guildhall

Middlesex St

ALDGATE

Lothbury Gallery

Bank of England Museum

Whitechapel Art Gallery

Aldgate

Threadneedle St

BANK

Cornhill

Leadenhall St

King William St

Nelson Collection

Gracechurch St

Cannon Street

MONUMENT

Fenchurch St

FENCHURCH ST.

CANNON ST.

The Monument

Eastcheap

Gt Tower St

TOWER HILL

Upper Thames St

EC3

Lower Thames St

London Br

Tower of London

Tower of London

River Thames

Southwark Cathedral

Tower Bridge

LONDON BRIDGE

Tooley Street

Borough High St

St Thomas St

George Inn

Bermondsey St

Tower Bridge Road

BOROUGH

London Glass Blowing Workshop

Long Lane

Druid St

Index

Index by type of attraction

Index by type of attraction

Alphabetical index

Alphabetical index